AF261017

COMMODUS

AND THE

FIVE GOOD EMPERORS

History and Allegory

By

Jasper Burns

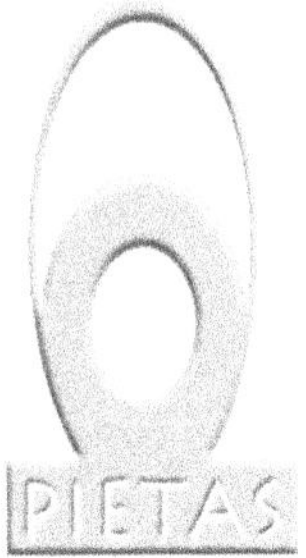

Pietas Publications
Copyright 2012

Coin portraits courtesy of Classical Numismatic Group, Inc.
www.cngcoins.com

Published by:

Pietas Publications
Waynesboro, Virginia, USA
web: www.jasperburns.com
email: pietas@jasperburns.com

COMMODUS

AND THE
FIVE GOOD EMPERORS

Contents

INTRODUCTION

Historians have long celebrated the "golden age" of the Roman Empire, when the so-called "five good emperors" held sway over a period of peace, prosperity, and personal freedom. This imperial "high noon", lasting from A.D. 96 to 180, embraced the reigns of Nerva, Trajan, Hadrian, Antoninus Pius, and Marcus Aurelius and ended with the reign of the "bad emperor" Commodus, son of Marcus Aurelius and villain of the movies "Gladiator" and "Fall of the Roman Empire". The ancient historian Cassius Dio famously claimed that his rule marked the end of the age of gold and the beginning of an age of "iron and rust" in the Roman world.

Each of the five consecutive rulers beginning with Nerva named his successor, and only Marcus Aurelius chose his own son - the others being adopted by their son-less predecessors. While all of the five good emperors seem to have been admirable men and competent rulers, they were very different in their personal traits and style of rule.

Nerva was a politician with no military experience whose shrewdness allowed him to survive close association with the tyrants Nero and Domitian as well as a military coup during his own reign. His successor Trajan was a man of action – a gifted warrior and administrator who had little interest in culture and was most at home while hunting or with the army. He adopted his cousin Hadrian – a sophisticated, highly educated intellectual and *bon vivant* whose knowledge of the world was unsurpassed. Hadrian's successor Antoninus Pius was a paragon of virtue who never left Italy during a reign marked by extreme attention to duty and detail. His son-in-law and successor Marcus Aurelius was a humble man and dedicated ruler whose true obsession was self-inquiry and the search for philosophical truth. In contrast, Marcus's son Commodus made a spectacle of himself through his flamboyant behavior, public displays of athletic skill, and claims to divinity.

No doubt, the conduct of these men was largely determined by their tastes and personalities as well as the particular circumstances of their reigns. However, it is interesting that the characters of the successive rulers trace a path for personal growth – from adaptability (Nerva) to activity (Trajan) to worldly knowledge (Hadrian) to virtue (Antoninus Pius) to wisdom (Marcus Aurelius) to an attempt at god consciousness (Commodus). In this sense, at least, Commodus' reign may be seen not as a departure from the path of his predecessors but as an attempted culmination.

The following pages present brief biographies of all six rulers followed by a series of imaginary letters from each emperor to his successor – and from Commodus to his deceased father. The premise of this exercise is that the characters of the 2nd century Roman emperors went through a development analogous to the maturing process of a single individual. And that this was partly due to observation of past mistakes and a chain of advice from emperor to emperor. This idea may be illustrated by an allegory:

> There was a young man who had to contend with unpredictable authority figures (Nerva under Nero and Domitian). He learned to stay on their good side through flattery, flexibility - even hypocrisy. He learned how to survive. However, when he became an independent man, answerable to no one (Trajan), he took responsibility for himself, became active, set goals, and made his mark on the world. When his success was assured and he entered middle age, he turned his mind to enjoyment and self-improvement (Hadrian) – he took up hobbies and cultivated new skills. He learned about the finer things in life. Eventually, as he aged, he lost interest in his new toys and tastes and began to prize virtue and an attitude of service to others above all else (Antoninus Pius). He lived simply and modestly, putting duty and the welfare of others first. Finally, in old age, he turned to the serious study of philosophy (Marcus Aurelius), striving to answer the big questions: who am I, why am I here, where am I going? Ultimately, believing that his soul was connected to the divine, he began to care less about propriety and duty and more about self-knowledge and god-realization. Ultimately, he followed the lead of saints and demigods and declared fearlessly that he was was divine; the son of god (Commodus). If his vision and understanding

were true, he became a saint. If he was delusional, he became mad. In either case, he would eventually be murdered by his own people.

Certainly, the successive emperors learned from the mistakes and advice of their predecessors; each new emperor striving to equal or surpass his forbearers while dealing with new circumstances and his personal limitations. In the case of Commodus, he had the additional pressure of trying to live up to the example of a real father who had scaled the heights as military leader, administrator, ruler, and philosopher. There was little he could do to surpass him - other than reach for the stars

The latter half of this book is a work of fiction that, in conjunction with the factual biographical sketches, may reveal some interesting contrasts and paradoxes in the lives of these rulers. Perhaps this study puts the reign and personality of Commodus in a context that sheds some light on why he broke the mold of the "good emperor" so spectacularly.

BIOGRAPHICAL SKETCHES

NERVA (reigned A.D. 96-98)

Marcus Cocceius Nerva was born at Narnia, 50 miles north of Rome, on November 8, probably in the year 30 during the reign of Tiberius, to whom he was distantly related. Nerva's father was a senator and wealthy lawyer, whose father had been a member of Tiberius' inner circle.

It is not known if Nerva ever married and there is no record of his having had children. Apparently, he had some ability as a poet - he was praised for his literary talents by Nero, who also wrote poetry. Nerva held some minor political posts in Rome and seems to have been a respected lawyer. However, he never served in the military or in provincial administration. Despite this, he became a key advisor to the emperors Nero, Vespasian, and Domitian.

In A.D. 65, Nerva played an important role in defeating an attempt to overthrow Nero (the Pisonian Conspiracy). He was probably involved in thwarting the revolt of Saturninus against Domitian in 89. On three occasions, he was awarded the consulship, the highest political office available to a private citizen - by Nero in 65, in 71 by Vespasian, and by Domitian in 90. It was a mark of exceptional distinction for someone outside the imperial family to be named consul three times.

Nerva must have possessed extraordinary political dexterity to prosper at the highest level under emperors as volatile as Nero and Domitian. Many men of his rank were eliminated as potential rivals or because their wealth was coveted or envied. Indeed, the story goes that, in A.D. 96 when Nerva was 65, the emperor Domitian decided to have him executed. However, the emperor was dissuaded when it was predicted by an astrologer that Nerva would die soon in any case.

It is probable that Nerva was part of the conspiracy that assassinated Domitian on September 18, 96 as he was named emperor by the Roman Senate on that same day. He was popular with his peers because of his experience, neutrality, affability, and proven political prowess. However, he had little support from the people and the assassination was deeply resented by the soldiers, who adored Domitian and had little regard for an old man with no military experience.

Because of his lack of support outside the Senate, Nerva's position was precarious. He tried to buy popularity by giving away large sums of money, lowering taxes, recalling exiles, and giving land grants to the poor. He even renamed Domitian's extravagant palace the "House of the People" and opened it for public use. He also made a show of his own frugality by selling off imperial possessions and living simply, in contrast to his predecessor. He tried to please all factions, prompting the historian Suetonius to write that "no one could do anything under Domitian; anyone could do anything under Nerva".

Despite Nerva's efforts to pacify them, the troops loyal to Domitian finally showed their resentment in violent action. Soldiers of the Praetorian Guard entered the palace and demanded the surrender for punishment of the men responsible for Domitian's murder. Nerva refused to acquiesce and was physically brushed aside – even when he offered his own neck to the armed soldiers in an attempt to shame them into withdrawing. The assassins were seized and brutally killed and Nerva was forced to publicly thank the praetorians for the deed.

Nerva's grasp on power was now at a dangerous low. In addition to his political troubles, he was in ill-health, often unable to keep his food down. His portraits reveal him to have been extremely thin and possibly frail at this stage of his life. However, the ever-nimble politician made a master stroke that stabilized his reign and satisfied his opponents.

On October 25, 97, he named the most respected military leader in the Empire – Marcus Ulpius Traianus (Trajan) – as his adopted son and heir. This brilliant choice (which may have been a foregone conclusion as Trajan had the power to take the throne by force if he desired) began a long period of remarkable prosperity, stability, and capable rule – and assured Nerva's reputation as the first of the "five good emperors". Later historians also praised him for being wise, calm, sensible, pragmatic, and moderate - and for managing to blend autocracy and individual freedom. He has also been called the ultimate "committee man" – a transitional figure rather than a dynamic leader.

Nerva died on January 27, 98 after an outburst of temper led to a fever (possibly a stroke) – an ironic end for a man whose self-control and diplomacy had enabled him to survive so many dangerous times and circumstances. He was deified by the Senate and his ashes were placed in the mausoleum of the emperor Augustus on the day of a solar eclipse.

TRAJAN (reigned A. D. 98-117)

Marcus Ulpius Traianus - the first Roman emperor who did not grow up in Italy - was born on September 18, most likely in the year 56 (or possibly a few years earlier). He was from the city of Italica in the province of Baetica in southern Spain and his wife, Pompeia Plotina, probably came from Nemausus (modern Nîmes, France) in southern Gaul.

The Romans' first experience of rule by provincials was a resounding success. Trajan was celebrated in his lifetime as *Optimus Princeps*, or "the best of princes", and Plotina became one of the most praised women in Roman history, honored for her dignity, simplicity, and many other virtues.

Trajan's father, also named Marcus Ulpius Traianus, commanded a legion under Vespasian during the First Jewish Revolt (A. D. 66-73). When Vespasian became emperor, he made the senior Trajan a consul and promoted his son to the Senate. The young Trajan, whose hero was Julius Caesar, pursued a military career, serving under his father in Syria and later in Germany.

Tall and well-built, Trajan had an even temper and agreeable nature. He grew prematurely gray, which seems only to have enhanced his impressive appearance. He was not artistically or intellectually inclined. He delighted in the soldier's life and enjoyed gladiatorial displays, hunting, and dining with friends. He often drank wine to excess, though he instructed his servants to stop serving him when he became drunk. Trajan also indulged a passion for young boys, a taste which was common and more or less acceptable in Trajan's time, especially in the Roman upper classes.

Trajan continued to climb the career ladder under the emperor

Domitian, who posted him to the command of a legion in Spain. In January of 89, Domitian showed his confidence by ordering Trajan to take his troops all the way to Germany (a journey of 700 miles) to put down the rebellion of a Roman general named Saturninus. The uprising was quashed before Trajan had arrived on the scene, but he was praised for his loyalty and the promptness of his response, which involved crossing both the Alps and the Pyrenees.

Domitian rewarded Trajan with a consulship for the year 91. This was the pinnacle of the professional career for a Roman senator and general and was very likely capped by an appointment to the governorship of one of the key northern provinces. Trajan was probably stationed near the Danube River when news came of Domitian's assassination (on Trajan's fortieth birthday) and Nerva's accession to the throne.

As an emperor without strong ties to the military, Nerva needed the support of the army, so he adopted Trajan, the most popular and respected soldier of the day, and designated him as his heir. He gave Trajan powers almost equal to his own and, when Nerva died, the new reign began without incident.

Trajan took the Roman Empire to new heights of prosperity and territorial expansion, ruling with a mildness and evenhandedness that became legendary. It became traditional after his death to wish that each succeeding emperor would prove to be "better than Trajan, more fortunate than Augustus".

Though he became emperor in January of 98, Trajan did not come to Rome until September of the following year, lingering in the northern provinces to strengthen their military defenses. He may also have been reluctant to leave the army camps and take his place in the center of Roman society. Trajan was a soldier by experience and inclination, with simple tastes and a strong sense of comraderie with his men. He is said to have known a great many of his soldiers not only by name, but also by their humorous camp nicknames.

In Rome, the new emperor made himself more accessible than any of his predecessors. Rather than remain aloof from his old friends, he visited them in their homes when they were sick and exchanged dinner invitations with them. When he traveled by carriage, he often took guests on board, though he usually preferred to walk from place to place. The imperial family dined publicly, welcoming visitors and mingling with their guests more or less as equals. Trajan was occasionally criticized for being too familiar with his subjects, but he said that he wished to behave towards others as he had wished previous emperors would behave towards him.

Trajan and his wife Plotina were childless, which may have inspired their special concern for the welfare of needy and maltreated children. He passed laws freeing abused sons from the control of their fathers and tightening the regulation of guardians. In ancient times, it was common for unwanted babies to be exposed, allowing anyone who wished to claim them, and raise them as their own. Trajan decreed that those abandoned babies who had been freeborn could assert their freedom as adults without having to repay their foster parents. The disadvantaged children of Italy also benefited from the *alimenta* system, which had been instituted as a government program under Nerva but was expanded by Trajan. When he lent large sums of money to rural districts in an effort to reverse the decline of Italian agriculture, he stipulated that the 5% interest on the loans would be used to feed poor children.

In A. D. 100, a consulship was awarded to Pliny the Younger (Gaius Plinius, born in 61 or 62), who expressed his appreciation to the Emperor in a speech of praise. Pliny later published an expanded version, known as the *Panegyricus*, which is one of our best sources of information about Trajan's reign.

There also exist some letters between Pliny and Trajan. The most famous of these concern Pliny's request for guidance from the Emperor regarding the treatment of Christians in the province of Bithynia (in northern Turkey), where Pliny was governor. Trajan's instructions: "these people must not be hunted out; if they are brought before you and the charge against them is proven, they must be punished, but in the case of anyone who denies that he is a Christian, and makes it clear that he is not by offering prayers to our gods, he is to be pardoned as a result of his repentance, however suspect his past conduct may be. But pamphlets circulated anonymously must play no part in any accusation. They create the worst sort of precedent and are quite out of keeping with the spirit of our age."

As adored and successful as Trajan was in Italy, the old soldier must have been secretly pleased when trouble with the neighboring kingdom of Dacia (roughly modern Romania) required him to join his army along the Danube. Between 101 and 106, the Emperor led the Roman legions in two major wars that ended with the destruction of the enemy and the addition of Dacia to the Roman Empire. The spoils of victory added no less than five million pounds of gold and ten million pounds of silver to Trajan's treasury. The celebration in Rome lasted for 123 days and involved the sacrifice of 11,000 animals and combats between 10,000 gladiators.

The booty from the Dacian wars allowed Trajan to embark on a spectacular building program. Besides the Forum and Column, he built or improved harbors, bridges, roads, aqueducts - even a shopping mall in the capital with 150 indoor shops. Triumphal arches were erected in many parts of the Empire. Trajan's name adorned so many buildings in Rome that he was compared to a vine or creeper.

Never before had the Roman Empire enjoyed such prosperity and military strength. By 112, its borders had expanded even further with the annexation of the Province of Arabia. It must have seemed that Trajan could do no wrong. The stability and prosperity he had achieved were so profound that it would be half a century before their erosion would become perceptible.

In the fall of 113, problems with Rome's longtime enemy Parthia required the aging emperor to head east and take the field of battle once again. Trajan's operations in the East would occupy him for the rest of his life.

The Parthian war brought Trajan his greatest triumphs and his greatest tragedies. His armies swept all before them, conquering Armenia and Mesopotamia and occupying Ctesiphon, the Parthian capital. At the mouth of the Tigris River on the Persian Gulf, the Emperor, now in his late fifties, watched a merchant ship sail for India and wished that he was as young as Alexander the Great had been so that he, too, could lead his army there. However, Trajan had already overextended himself. While he daydreamed at the Gulf, his new conquests were in rebellion, killing or expelling their Roman garrisons.

Trajan's forces were still trying to restore order in Parthia when news came of a serious revolt of the Jews living in Cyrene, Cyprus, and Alexandria. There was long-standing animosity between the Greek and Jewish populations in the eastern provinces, largely because of religious and cultural differences. The destruction of Jerusalem and its temple by Titus in 70 had left a legacy of Jewish resentment against the Romans as well. The historian Cassius Dio claims that the Jewish rebels massacred nearly half a million Greeks and Romans in Cyrene and Cyprus, and committed other atrocities in Egypt before the revolt could be put down.

Trajan tried desperately to regain control of the situation. Faced with a new Parthian invasion of Armenia, he was forced to acknowledge client-kings there and in Parthia itself rather than formally annex them to the Empire as he had hoped to do. Then his attempt to recapture the desert fortress of Hatra, crucial to the control of Mesopotamia, ended in failure. The siege of this city exposed Trajan and his men to thirst, terrible weather, and hosts of flies that covered their food and drink and spread disease.

Clearly, the Emperor's luck had changed. He wintered in Antioch at the end of 116, planning to march into Mesopotamia again the following year. However, by the spring of 117, his health had begun to fail. Trajan fell ill soon after the failure at Hatra - perhaps a late victim of the flies - and suffered a stroke that left him partially paralyzed. His extremities became swollen and he suffered from other ominous symptoms.

Trajan set sail for Rome in July of 117, leaving Syria and his dreams of eastern conquest behind for good. He imagined that he was being poisoned, and blamed this for his sickness. Three hundred miles into the journey, off the coast of what is now southern Turkey, Trajan's health took a serious turn for the worse. His ship put in at the nearest port, the city of Selinus (afterwards known as Trajanopolis), where he died, on or about the 9th of August, not quite 61 years of age. Trajan's body was taken back to Syria, where it was cremated.

After his death, the Senate received a letter from Trajan, written from his deathbed, naming his cousin and ward, Publius Aelius Hadrianus (Hadrian), as his adopted son and heir. However, Trajan's wife Plotina had signed the document rather than the emperor, presumably because his paralysis prevented him from writing. This raised the possibility that Hadrian had not been the Emperor's choice at all, but Plotina's. However, at the time of Trajan's death, Hadrian was governor of the critical province of Syria with a large army at his command. Clearly, Trajan trusted him to handle the dangerous situation in the East when his own health was failing. Also, the Emperor had given Hadrian a diamond that he had received from Nerva, perhaps to signify his designation as successor. There is little doubt that Hadrian was Trajan's choice to succeed him; he had left no one else in a position to challenge for the throne.

HADRIAN (reigned 117-138)

Publius Aelius Hadrianus (Hadrian), born on January 24, 76, was the son of Trajan's first cousin on his father's side. When Hadrian lost his father at the age of ten, he became the ward of Trajan and another man. There are reports that Trajan was often displeased with the young Hadrian because of his extravagant lifestyle and frequent indebtedness. However, the emperor's wife Plotina took a deep interest in the young man and helped arranged his marriage to Trajan's great-niece Sabina in 100 with the support of the girl's mother and grandmother. This marriage to Sabina was a clear sign of imperial favor and was followed by numerous honors, including the consulship in 108.

Soon after his marriage to Sabina, Hadrian was elevated to the Senate. His travels and official assignments under Trajan took him to various parts of the Empire, including Pannonia on the Danube River, Greece, Asia Minor, and Syria. He was in Syrian Antioch in 117 when Trajan died and Hadrian became emperor.

Immediately after his accession, Hadrian alienated certain hawkish Roman senators by relinquishing Trajan's conquests in the East, thus depriving them of lucrative administrative posts in the new territories. Then, before he had even arrived in Rome, four distinguished senators were executed for plotting Hadrian's overthrow. Though he swore publicly that he was not responsible for these deaths and that he would never put a senator to death without a proper trial, the damage to his reputation had been done.

Hadrian was one of the most talented and active rulers in history. He was tall, robust, and elegant in his dress and grooming, with fair skin and piercing, close-set, gray-blue eyes that were "full of light." He wore a neatly trimmed beard in the Greek style (which set the fashion for emperors for the next century) and had his hair curled with a comb, as Nero and Domitian had done. He was probably the best educated of all Roman emperors, and the most enamored of Greek culture and history. He dressed in Greek clothing in private, even when in Italy. In fact, the only known statue of a Roman emperor in Greek attire is of Hadrian.

Hadrian's array of talents and cultivated abilities is astonishing. He was a gifted poet, writer, painter, and sculptor, an innovative architect, master astrologer, accomplished mathematician, singer, and musician (specializing in the flute). His memory was prodigious; like Trajan, he was able to remember the names of countless soldiers in his army. He loved mountain climbing and was an avid hunter, risking his life in the pursuit of boars, bears, and lions. His mastery of the military arts and sciences ranged from the broadest defensive strategy to the tiniest details of a foot soldier's equipment and battle tactics.

However, Hadrian could be unpredictable and exasperating. Though usually affable and accessible to the common man, he was sometimes aloof and arrogant. He was jealous of experts in the many fields where he possessed some expertise and intolerant of rivals, though he rewarded and supported them as readily as he humiliated them. According to an anecdote in the *Historia Augusta*, the skilled rhetorician Favorinus was once criticized for not defending himself when the Emperor had falsely accused him of misusing a word. Favorinus' response was revealing: "You are mistaken, my friends, in urging me not to consider the commander of 30 legions the most learned of men."

Hadrian seems to have measured himself against some of the most formidable minds of his day. Besides Favorinus, he probably matched wits with the brilliant Stoic philosopher Epictetus, the famous Greek writer and biographer Plutarch, the noted historian Arrian, the influential Greek sophist Polemo, and the accomplished architect Apollodorus of Damascus, designer of Trajan's magnificent Forum in Rome.

Hadrian could be alternately playful and stern, merciful and cruel, modest and vainglorious. Many of his qualities and interests seem contradictory, but also show an unparalleled versatility. For example, he was a practical man with a strong interest in astrology, mysticism, and magic. Though a calculating politician, he was also a romantic dreamer, given to sentimental outbursts that opened him up to ridicule. He was a dandified *bon vivant* who delighted in lavish banquets and yet seemed perfectly content with the harsh living conditions and simple food of the common Roman soldier. Though a refined, highly educated intellectual, Hadrian loved to mingle naked with the common folk at the public baths, sharing their coarsest jokes.

Hadrian relished a good dinner party, where he could enjoy philosophical discussion as well as musical, literary, and theatrical performances. As important lights in Roman society, he and his wife Sabina attended and gave countless banquets.

Hadrian was first and foremost a lover of all things Greek. As a young man, he earned the nickname *"Graeculus"* ("the Greekling") for his obsession with Greek culture. From his personal appearance to his religious tastes, he patterned himself after the heroes of classical and archaic Greece. He also participated in the Hellenic custom of man-boy love, in which an adult man entered into a romantic, sexual, socially sanctioned relationship with an adolescent boy. Though this practice was alien to Roman tradition, it had become well established among the upper classes by Hadrian's time. As we shall see, Hadrian's attachment to one young man, a Bithynian named Antinous, would become famous.

Hadrian's long, prosperous reign was marked by a series of grand tours, during which he visited at least 38 and probably all but one of the 44 provinces of the Empire. His travels occupied nearly two thirds of his 21 years on the throne. The imperial retinue included Sabina and other members of the royal family and their friends and senatorial advisors, as well as poets, pages, and hunting partners for the Emperor.

The visits to the provinces were far more than sightseeing trips. The entourage also included architects, builders, and stone masons, for Hadrian restored old buildings and built new ones wherever he went. He also founded cities and encouraged local artistic, cultural, and religious institutions. In fact, the Emperor's activities prompted the Greek writer Pausanias, writing a generation later, to credit Hadrian with "having done more to increase the happiness of each of his subjects than any other ruler in history."

Hadrian inspected and drilled the army in the provinces he visited. Surviving examples of his speeches to the troops reveal a meticulous attention to detail and concern for morale. He concentrated on defining and defending the existing boundaries of the Empire, constructing permanent barriers on several borders. These included an extensive wooden palisade along the German frontier, stone and mud brick walls along the southern boundaries in Africa, and, of course, "Hadrian's Wall" in northern Britain. Hadrian's Wall was 14 feet high and built of stone, with a small fortress every mile and two lookout towers in between. It extended for 73 miles from coast to coast, with a 40-mile extension along the western shoreline.

Hadrian said that the administration of the Empire should "combine justice with human kindness." He backed up his words with numerous edicts that were intended to protect his subjects, especially those most vulnerable. For example, he passed several laws protecting the rights of slaves, making it illegal for them to be killed by their owners. Sweatshops for slave or free workers were banned and slaves could not be sold to fight as gladiators or to work as prostitutes unless their owners could show just cause.

Unfortunately, at least one of Hadrian's well-intentioned edicts was spectacularly ill-advised. When Hadrian made circumcision illegal, considering it to be a barbarous practice similar to castration, it sparked a rebellion in Judaea (132), known as the Second Jewish

Revolt, that cost at least half a million lives before it was put down.

Hadrian's building projects were numerous and prodigious. He had a passion for architecture, and the means to indulge it. His restored version of the Pantheon in Rome remains one of the most magnificent buildings in the world, with a soaring dome 142 feet high. His villa at Tibur (modern Tivoli) near Rome was certainly one of the most extravagant personal residences ever built. This complex of gracefully designed structures covered an area of 1000 by 500 yards. It included several dining halls, numerous guestrooms, theaters, baths, and countless fountains and pools - even underground corridors intended to represent Hades.

The villa was everywhere decorated with colorful paintings, mosaics, and innumerable sculptures. These were of such quality and variety that the residence has been called the world's first museum. No imperial couple collected works of art more extensively than Hadrian and Sabina, and no society in history has had a greater enthusiasm for art than the Roman Empire.

Hadrian spent as much of his time as possible in Greece, visiting the shrines of her magnificent past and striving to promote the glory and influence of Greek culture. He embellished city after city with temples, libraries, and other buildings. Hadrian even founded a Greek-style university in Rome, the first such institution in the western part of the Empire. He also established a confederation of Greek cities - the *Panhellenion* - that revived the ancient dream of a united Greek world. Perhaps the most personally significant of Hadrian's experiences in Greece - shared enthusiastically by Sabina and her sister Matidia - was initiation into the Mysteries of Eleusis.

The most famous member of Hadrian's entourage in Egypt was his boyfriend, Antinous. Hadrian made no effort to hide his extreme attachment to this young man, who was probably born around the year 110. As numerous portraits of him show, Antinous was physically beautiful and seems to have personified for Hadrian the Greek ideal of male perfection in body, mind, and spirit. He joined the Emperor on his travels and hunting expeditions and became an established member of the imperial court. Other Roman emperors had pursued their love of boys without scandal and there is no indication of the relationship being ridiculed during Hadrian's lifetime. What set Antinous apart from previous boyfriends of Roman emperors was what happened after his death.

Less than a month before the visit to the Colossus of Memnon, the imperial party was traveling up the Nile by boat when Antinous drowned under mysterious circumstances. The Emperor insisted in his memoirs (which have not survived) that it was an accidental death and nothing more. However, the extreme honors paid to the young man, including deification and the founding of the city of Antinoopolis where he had died, encouraged a variety of fantastic rumors. It was claimed that he had been sacrificed or had sacrificed himself for the benefit of the Emperor, his life being an offering to extend Hadrian's time on earth.

Whatever the actual circumstances, there is no doubt that Antinous was deified and became the object of a popular new cult. His supposed resurrection was believed to offer the same sort of hope for the faithful that was to be found in Eleusis or the stories of Dionysos and Jesus. The parallels to Jesus were so close that later Christian writers targeted Antinous for criticism, calling him an unworthy rival of Christ.

Perhaps the most enduring legacy of Antinous' life and death was an outpouring of highly artistic portraits of him. Hadrian was said to have wept "like a woman" after the loss of his beloved, and he commemorated Antinous in at least 22 statues that have been discovered at his villa at Tibur (only two of Hadrian's wife Sabina have been found there).

The childless Hadrian was forced to adopt his successor, a task he put off until late in his life. His first choice, announced in 136 when the Emperor was 60, was a handsome young noble to whom he gave the name Aelius Caesar. However, Aelius died of tuberculosis on New Year's Day, 138 and Hadrian was forced to find another man. He promptly selected a very distinguished 51 year-old senator with the ample name of Titus Aurelius Fulvus Boionius Arrius Antoninus. Reluctant to assume the purple, Antoninus deliberated for a whole month before accepting the honor.

Hadrian's death at the age of 62, probably from heart failure, seems to have been slow and painful. He reportedly longed for death and tried unsuccessfully to get his attendants to put him out of his misery. The historian Cassius Dio wrote that he finally succumbed when he abandoned his regimen and over-indulged in unsuitable food and drink.

After Hadrian's death on July 10, 138, Antoninus assumed power and asked the Roman Senate to deify his predecessor. However, the deceased emperor was so unpopular that the request was denied. The senators even threatened to cancel the decrees of Hadrian, as had been done after the deaths of "bad" emperors such as Caligula and Domitian. Antoninus insisted on due honors being paid to Hadrian, pointing out that if his acts were cancelled, then his own adoption and right to rule would become null and void. The Senate relented, and, probably because of his dutiful efforts on Hadrian's behalf, bestowed the name *Pius* ("the pious one") on the new emperor.

As it happened, Hadrian had not been content with naming his own successor - he named Antoninus' successors as well. He had required the new Caesar to adopt as his sons and heirs Lucius Verus, the 8 year-old son of Aelius Caesar, his first choice as successor, and Marcus Aurelius, Antoninus 17 year-old nephew. (Antoninus' own two sons had probably died by this time, or passed away soon after Antoninus came to power.) Hadrian's arrangements for the future were inspired; Antoninus and Marcus Aurelius proved to be two of the finest rulers in history.

ANTONINUS PIUS (reigned 138-161)

Titus Aurelius Fulvus Boionius Arrius Antoninus was born 20 miles south of Rome on September 19, 86. He grew up at his family home at Lorium, ten miles west of the capital, where he would build a palace in later years. Both of his parent's families were wealthy and distinguished and seem to have come from southern Gaul - perhaps from Nemausus (modern Nîmes, France), the home of Trajan's wife Plotina.

Antoninus was tall, bearded, and physically strong, with a noble bearing but unpretentious manners. His numerous portraits show a mild, earnest-looking man, with pleasant features and a yearning look that is reminiscent of later depictions of the Christian saints. The written accounts of Antoninus' life are short on historical detail, but long on praise for his many good qualities. His contemporaries described him as nothing less than a paragon of virtue. He was friendly, intelligent, thrifty, forgiving, peace loving, prudent, compassionate, and kind. Antoninus was curious about many things and enjoyed hunting, fishing, and attending the theater. He was praised for treating the Senate with respect and for reducing the imperial pomp "to the utmost simplicity." He lived modestly, even participating in the grape harvest like a private citizen.

Nevertheless, Antoninus knew how to give a good show. The marriage of his younger daughter Faustina to Marcus Aurelius was a major spectacle. Also, in celebration of the 900th anniversary of the founding of Rome, he gave lavish games in the arena, involving elephants, rhinos, crocodiles, and hippos, and as many as 100 lions and tigers in one event.

Antoninus seems to have possessed a dry sense of humor. He once summoned a man named Apollonius from Chalcedon in Bithynia (in northern Turkey) to tutor his nephew Marcus Aurelius in Rome. When Apollonius was asked to come to the palace to meet his student, he replied, "A master should not come to a pupil, but a pupil to the master." Antoninus laughed and said, "It was easier for Apollonius to come from Chalcedon to Rome than from his house to the palace." On another occasion, when a foppish philosopher complained that the Emperor was not paying attention to him, Antoninus responded, "I am paying attention, and I know you well. You are the fellow who is always arranging his hair, cleaning his teeth and polishing his nails, and always smells of myrrh."

His compassionate nature is shown by a remark made when the palace servants admonished the young Marcus for shedding tears over the death of a tutor: "Let him be human, for neither philosophy nor imperial power takes away feelings." Antoninus often quoted a line attributed to the Roman hero Scipio: "I would rather save a single citizen than slay a thousand foes." His concern for the slave population of the Empire was shown by edicts forbidding their cruel or abusive treatment.

The highest praise of Antoninus comes from those who knew him best of all. For example, the rhetorician Marcus Cornelius Fronto, who was Antoninus' friend and the tutor of his adopted sons, called the Emperor a "god-like man," whose outstanding qualities excelled those of all other rulers. Marcus Aurelius, writing privately rather than for public consumption, exhorted himself "to be the disciple of Antoninus in all things" and to emulate his "rationality, even temper, piety, serenity, sweetness, patience, forbearance, simplicity, industry, and open-mindedness."

No wonder Antoninus was more genuinely mourned than any other Roman emperor. Two hundred years after his passing, the Roman historian Ammianus Marcellinus referred to him simply as "Antoninus the Good."

Antoninus' public career contrasted sharply with those of Trajan and Hadrian in its lack of travel and military experience. He is only known to have left Italy once in his life, sometime between the years 133 and 136, to serve as the proconsul (governor) of the province of Asia (modern western Turkey).

There are a couple of interesting stories about Antoninus' sojourn in Asia that reflect his humble and forgiving nature. When his party arrived in Smyrna, they were settled in the finest house in the city, which happened to belong to the orator, Antonius Polemo. Polemo, who was out of town at the time, was said to think so highly of himself that "he talked to the gods as his equals." When he unexpectedly returned late at night and found his house occupied, he raised such a fuss that Antoninus was forced to vacate the premises. On another occasion, when traveling by carriage on a narrow mountain road, Antoninus was nearly forced into a ditch by the carriage of another rich, arrogant orator. This man, named Herodes Atticus, was even said to have struck Antoninus during the incident. Despite these indignities, Antoninus bore ill will towards neither man and honored them both when he became emperor.

Antoninus lost his wife Faustina only two years after he became emperor. She was most likely in her early forties. Antoninus was heartbroken. He showed his undying devotion to his wife throughout the remaining 20 years of his rule by continuing to honor her memory in a variety of ways. Faustina was deified and called *Diva Faustina* on the enormous imperial coinage that was issued in her memory - more than for any other empress. She was associated on these coins with a variety of goddesses, but particularly with those that were concerned with the afterlife. Many bore the legend *Aeternitas,* referring to Faustina's eternal life among the gods in Heaven. Remarkably, this coinage continued to be issued in unabated abundance throughout her husband's long reign.

Antoninus further honored his wife's memory by establishing a charitable organization for the benefit of poor Italian girls, called the *Puellae Faustinianae,* or "Faustina's girls." It provided financial support, free education, and perhaps even dowries for underprivileged young women. Antoninus' love for his wife and grief at her passing cannot be doubted, but public displays of devotion are perhaps less convincing than private words. It is fortunate that a letter of his survives, written to his friend Cornelius Fronto a couple of years after Faustina's death. In thanking Fronto for compliments to the Emperor in a speech to the Senate, Antoninus expresses his particular gratitude for remarks made in honor of "my Faustina." He writes that "In truth, I would rather live with her on Gyara (a desolate island of exile) than in the palace without her."

As Antoninus grew older, he became stooped and had to have willow boards strapped to his chest to straighten his posture. His old age was enlivened by a horde of grandchildren and an exemplary relationship with Marcus Aurelius, his devoted nephew and son-in-law, who shouldered more and more of the burden of rule as the years passed. On March 7, 161, Antoninus died at the age of 74 at Lorium, his childhood home, reportedly from overindulging in Swiss cheese. It is reported that his final moments were spent complaining about the state of the Empire and expressing his anger toward certain kings.

MARCUS AURELIUS (reigned 161-180)

Marcus Aurelius was born on April 26, 121 into an extremely prestigious and wealthy family. As a young boy, his excellent qualities attracted the attention of the Emperor Hadrian, who called him *Verissimus,* or "truest". Marcus was taught by some of the most accomplished men of his time and was early and profoundly attracted to philosophy. The personal writings of his mature years, which have come down to us as his "Meditations," reveal much about his character.

As a youth, Marcus was fond of literature, painting, and sports. He learned to hunt on horseback and to fight in full armor, though he was somewhat frail and prone to ill health. Even after being elevated to imperial rank, he was unassuming in his dress and demeanor. His portraits reveal a handsome young man, with a tousled mass of curly hair, large, protruding, soulful eyes, and a small mouth with cupid's bow lips.

We probably have a better record of Marcus Aurelius' changing appearance through life than of any other person from ancient times. The numerous portraits that survive follow him from his teens to old age and reveal the toll that his responsibilities and personal disappointments took on him. When he reached manhood, Marcus grew a long beard, reflecting his self-identification as a philosopher.

Marcus Aurelius was drawn to the philosophical school known as Stoicism (founded by Zeno in Athens, Greece in the late fourth-century B. C.). As a Stoic, Marcus believed that the Divine inhabited each human being as the soul, and was also revealed in the form of the natural universe. Therefore, he held that the virtuous life consisted of reverent and dutiful service to mankind while embracing one's worldly circumstances as the gift of God. He also believed that spiritual upliftment could be obtained through wisdom and equanimity, acquired through self-control and the contemplation of truth.

Marcus believed in the gods as different aspects of the one divine principle. As he put it: "…with respect to the gods, from what I constantly experience of their power, I comprehend that they exist and I venerate them." However, he did not necessarily believe that the actions of human beings could influence them. Nevertheless, he actively supported and participated in the rituals of religion, and received initiation into the Mysteries of Demeter and Persephone at Eleusis. He believed that the individual was uplifted and the cohesion of the state was enhanced through religious practices.

In the spring of 145, Marcus married his first cousin Faustina, the daughter of Antoninus Pius. This event caused great excitement in Rome; it was certainly the most notable wedding in an imperial family since the union of Nero and the emperor Claudius' daughter Octavia nearly a century before. Antoninus officiated at the ceremony and coins were issued showing the groom on one side and the bride on the other.

On November 30, 147, Faustina gave birth to a girl named Domitia Faustina, the first of at least fourteen (and probably fifteen) children that she and Marcus would have together over the next 23 years. (Six girls and eight boys (including two sets of twins) are recorded with reasonable certainty.) Faustina's second set of twins (one of whom was Commodus) were born on August 31, 161, nearly six months after Antoninus Pius died and their father became emperor.

Marcus Aurelius established a precedent by naming the younger Lucius Verus as his co-emperor, equal to him in power in every way, except that Marcus alone held the post of chief priest *(Pontifex Maximus)*. This arrangement, which restored Hadrian's original plan, was successful because Lucius Verus deferred to his older colleague.

Marcus Aurelius was as beloved as any of his predecessors among the so-called "five good emperors". However, while they had presided over periods of success and prosperity at home and abroad, Marcus' popularity was won and maintained through a series of hardships and disasters, which began soon after his accession.

In the autumn of 161, a flood did serious damage to the city of Rome, followed by a famine that affected much of Italy. Meanwhile, the king of the Parthian Empire invaded the Roman client kingdom of Armenia and placed his own man on the throne. When the Roman governor of Cappadocia marched a legion into Armenia in response, his army was massacred and he committed suicide. As if on cue, hostile tribes on the frontiers of Britain and Germany took advantage of the situation and took arms against Rome. The German tribesmen even made minor forays into Roman territory.

An advantage of having two emperors was that one could take the field in a military crisis while the other remained at Rome to administer the Empire. In 162, Marcus sent the more vigorous Lucius Verus to answer the Parthian challenge. Handpicked generals were also dispatched to Britain and Germany to deal with the lesser dangers there. A series of Roman victories was won in the East by Lucius' generals (particularly Avidius Cassius, whom we shall meet again) and security was gradually restored.

The situation on the northern frontier proved far more dangerous. By the end of the year, the Germans had again crossed the northern border. The Roman army repelled the invaders, but the situation had become critical. Then came a serious outbreak of plague, presumably brought into the Empire by the veterans of Lucius' eastern armies as they returned from the Parthian War. The exact nature of the pestilence is unknown (smallpox and Bubonic plague have been suggested), but it raged throughout the eastern two-thirds of the Empire for the next 20 years, hitting the army and city dwellers especially hard. In Rome, perhaps as many as 2,000 people died per day at the peak of the epidemic, their bodies carried off in wagons and carts.

Most Romans believed that misfortunes such as these signaled the displeasure of the gods and foretold future calamities. Accordingly, Marcus called upon the priests of the state religion to perform special religious ceremonies in order to soothe the people and mollify the gods. Unfortunately, this spiritual remedy for the Empire's troubles had its indirect victims. The Christians, whose numbers were still relatively small, refused to participate in the public sacrifices. To Marcus and many of his subjects, this was tantamount to treason.

Sacrifice to the *genius,* or spirit, of the emperor and to the gods of the Roman state were the equivalent of pledging allegiance to the Empire. Refusal to do so was seen as more than religious nonconformity; it was disloyalty and the rejection of civic duty. In the prevailing atmosphere of fear and uncertainty, the non-cooperation of the Christians was viewed as an internal threat - almost a form of rebellion. The response was sporadic persecution, sanctioned but apparently not instigated by the Emperor, in which numerous Christians were killed.

The persecution of Christians has stained the reputation of Marcus Aurelius. However, he saw them as a collection of stubborn, overly dramatic exhibitionists, whose refusal to cooperate with his policies threatened Roman society at a time of extreme peril. His contempt for them may be more understandable in light of the stories he must have heard about them. For example, the sacrament of communion, in which Christians were said to drink the blood and eat the flesh of their deity, was sometimes misunderstood as a cannibalistic feast.

The danger of a renewed barbarian attack on the northern provinces had become so acute that Marcus decided both emperors were needed at the front. In the spring of 168, he and Lucius Verus left Rome to inspect and strengthen the Empire's defenses. The empress Faustina may have accompanied her husband on this tour; at least she seems to have been with him on his return journey through northern Italy in January 169. It was on this return trip that Lucius Verus suffered a sudden stroke in his carriage, dying three days later at the age of 39. This stunning loss must have only increased the public's sense of foreboding.

By 169, it was clear to Marcus Aurelius that a major war with the northern barbarians was inevitable. In preparation, he enlisted slaves, gladiators, and even semi-civilized bandits into the army – desperate measures made necessary because of the number of troops lost to disease and the seriousness of the threat. Reluctant to increase taxes in these uneasy times, Marcus auctioned off many of his household treasures to raise money, including some of Faustina's silken, gold-embroidered robes and her jewelry. Marcus told the Senate that "even the house we live in is yours."

In 170, the Roman army launched a pre-emptive strike across the northern frontier. To the horror of Romans everywhere, it met with a shocking defeat and was answered with a barbarian invasion of the Empire. The dam had finally broken. German invaders streamed deep into Roman territory, even besieging the city of Aquileia in northeastern Italy, only 300 miles from Rome itself. Not since the end of the second-century B. C. had a foreign enemy set foot on Italian soil.

In Greece, the famous shrine of Eleusis near Athens was destroyed. Everywhere the invaders went, the loss of life and damage to property were severe. Beyond mere looting, the German tribesmen were desperate to settle in the Empire in order to escape war-like tribes that were invading their lands from the north. Even German women joined their men in fighting against the Romans - this was a matter of survival.

Through tremendous Roman effort, the barbarians were gradually beaten back over a period of two years and the Empire's boundaries were restored. However, Marcus was forced to allow large numbers of Germans to settle under supervision on Roman territory, and he would spend the remainder of his life fighting wars and trying to maintain order along the northern frontier.

After their hard-won victory over the German invaders, the Roman soldiers requested a cash reward from the Emperor. Demonstrating his courage and high principles, Marcus refused, saying that this money "would be wrung from the blood of your parents and kinsmen." He also insisted that the fate of his regime did not depend on the Roman army; but on the will of Heaven. This rebuff of the troops involved some measure of risk on the Emperor's part, but, as Cassius Dio said, "nothing could force Marcus Aurelius to do anything that was inconsistent with his character."

It was during these years, while he was stationed at his northern military outposts, that Marcus composed his famous "Meditations." These extraordinary writings, written in Greek, show the Emperor to have been a wise, conscientious, and thoroughly humble and decent man. They reveal his struggle to apply philosophy to the conduct of his life, ever mindful of his mortality. Marcus was determined to do his duty and to avoid being corrupted by the temptations of power. The "Meditations" continue to instruct and inspire people to this day.

The Emperor's health was often poor, and early in 175, while he was at his base of Sirmium on the River Save (in modern Serbia), he became so ill that it was feared he would not recover. There are even hints that the Emperor considered committing suicide, viewed as an acceptable act under certain circumstances by the Stoics. His wife Faustina was with him at the time and must have been deeply concerned, not only for the welfare of her husband, but also for their family. Her son, Commodus, was only 13 and still too young to succeed to the throne.

It was at this inopportune moment that news came of a serious revolt within the Empire. Avidius Cassius, a hero of the Parthian war under Lucius Verus and now governor of Syria, had proclaimed himself emperor. He was a close friend of Marcus Aurelius and apparently acted in the belief that the Emperor was dead. All of the eastern provinces south of Asia Minor joined Cassius, including Egypt.

Marcus was heartbroken. Not only had his friend and one of his most capable generals deserted him, but the rebellion forced him into a hasty settlement with the Germans, just when he seemed close to a more permanent solution. He summoned Commodus from Rome, had him initiated prematurely into legal manhood, and officially proclaimed his son heir to the throne. This was intended to forestall Cassius from taking power should Marcus die before Cassius had been subdued. Marcus then prepared to meet the usurper's challenge, but before his army was even ready to march, word came that Cassius had been killed by his own soldiers. The rebellion had lasted only a little more than three months.

After the death of Cassius, Marcus decided to visit the eastern provinces, taking Faustina, Commodus, and other family members with him. The party left Sirmium by the end of July 175, sailed to the Danube, crossed the Balkans into Thrace, and traveled across what is now northern Turkey. The journey continued southeast during the winter to the foothills of Mount Taurus and the village of Halala in the province of Cappadocia, where Faustina sickened and died in late 175.

Marcus Aurelius honored his wife of thirty years in a eulogy and established a new order of underprivileged girls to be supported by the State as a tribute to her. This order, like the similar institution dedicated to her mother, was called the *puellae Faustinianae* ("Faustina's girls"). Cassius Dio states that Marcus wrote the Senate immediately after his wife's death, begging them not to execute any senators implicated in Cassius' rebellion, "as if through this he might be consoled for losing her." He may also have sought comfort in the Mysteries of Eleusis, into which Marcus and Commodus were initiated in September, 176, only months after Faustina's death.

Marcus Aurelius, aged 58, passed away on March 17, 180, probably at his northern base of Vindobona (modern Vienna, Austria). It was recorded that he welcomed death – and even hastened it by abstaining from food and drink. Also, that he banished all from his deathbed, lest they catch his disease, which may have been the plague. His final watchword for his tribune was "Go to the rising sun; I am already setting." His 19 year-old son Commodus, who had been a co-emperor since 177, now became sole emperor.

As Commodus would prove to be unpopular with the senators, whose version of history survives best, Marcus Aurelius has been blamed for abandoning the tradition established by his four predecessors of selecting the best available man to succeed him. It has been charged that he let his paternal affection for Commodus overrule his better judgment. This is nonsense; Marcus was the first emperor since Vespasian even to have a son who *could* succeed him. Any other choice would almost certainly have led to civil war, especially as Commodus had served as co-emperor for five years before Marcus died.

COMMODUS (reigned 177-192)

Lucius Aurelius Commodus, born August 31, 161, was the 10th child of Marcus Aurelius. His twin brother Antoninus died at the age of four. By the age of 5, Commodus had been named Caesar as the eldest surviving son of the emperor and the obvious heir to the throne.

Commodus' mother was Faustina the Younger, the daughter of Antoninus Pius. After her death, she was accused of numerous infidelities, including an affair with a gladiator who was rumored to be Commodus' real father. These charges belonged to a tradition that arose among the students and associates of her enemy, the influential sophist Herodes Atticus. Faustina was probably too busy as the mother of at least 14 children for such behavior. Even more persuasive in her defense are her husband's own words, written for himself in his *Meditations*: "Thank the gods that I have been blessed with a wife so docile, so affectionate, so genuine."

There is a story, told long after Commodus' death by a hostile historian, that at the age of 11 he ordered for an attendant to be thrown into the furnace for letting his bath water get cold (a sheepskin was burned instead to make Commodus think that his command had been obeyed). If indeed he was a spoiled brat, it may have been because his father was away from Rome for much of his childhood. To counter this negative impression are remarks by Cassius Dio that Commodus was not wicked by nature and would grow into the most guileless of men. He is described as extremely handsome, with a well-proportioned body (other than a prominent growth in his groin area – possibly a hernia), flashing eyes, and curly, golden hair that seemed like a heavenly halo in the sunlight. Commodus was left-handed and proud of it.

Marcus Aurelius saw to it that Commodus was educated by the finest teachers and probably hoped to prepare his son gradually for the responsibilities that awaited him. However, the revolt of Avidius Cassius in 175 forced him to catapult Commodus into premature manhood as a precaution against usurpers. By the age of 17, Commodus had already celebrated a triumph in Rome, become a consul and co-emperor with his father, and was a married man. He was only 19 when Marcus Aurelius died and he became sole emperor - the first ever to have been born during his father's reign and the first to succeed his natural father to the throne in a century.

After his accession, Commodus abandoned Marcus Aurelius' plan to expand the Empire northward. Most modern historians agree that this was probably a wise move as the land to be annexed was too vast and populous and the cost of conquest too high. Peace was made with the barbarians on terms that were very favorable to Rome and the Danube frontier would remain stable for the next 30 years. It may even be that Marcus Aurelius had decided in favor of this shift in policy before he died. Commodus continued to rely heavily on his father's advisors and there is no sign that they opposed the move. However, it made Commodus unpopular among the many senators who saw territorial expansion as a route to lucrative postings for themselves.

Opposition in the Roman Senate was exploited in 182 by Commodus' sister Lucilla, who, with co-conspirators, including her cousin Quadratus, planned to assassinate the young emperor. They may have intended to replace him with Lucilla's husband Tiberius Claudius Pompeianus (who was apparently unaware of the plot). The conspirators engaged Lucilla's nephew, a hot-headed young senator named Quintianus, to murder Commodus in public. Armed with a dagger, Quintianus met Commodus at the entrance to the Colosseum – but spent too much time telling the Emperor that it was the Senate who sent him his death. Before he could strike, the imperial guards had disarmed him and taken him into custody.

Lucilla was sent to the island of Capri and eventually executed – the same fate that would soon befall Commodus' only wife, Bruttia Crispina. Crispina's alleged crime was adultery. After his wife's passing, Commodus would never remarry and there is no record of his having any children. However, he reportedly took a number of mistresses (one source says 300). His favorite concubine was named Marcia, formerly the mistress of the conspirator Quadratus. Commodus is said to have treated Marcia as his legal wife and even almost as an empress. She was reportedly on very good terms with the Christians, persuading Commodus to follow a benign policy towards them. She even arranged for him to recall to Rome a number of Christians who had been exiled to the island of Sardinia.

Commodus was religiously-inclined from a young age. At the age of 14 or 15, he was initiated with his father into the Mysteries of Demeter and Persephone at Eleusis near Athens, Greece. He was drawn to the Egyptian goddess Isis, even shaving his head for her rites and joining in her processions. He carried a wooden statue of Anubis, the jackal-headed god, with which he reportedly touched worshippers on the head as if to bless them. He also showed interest in the cults of the goddess Ma Bellona and the Persian god Mithras, favored by many in the army. However, as future events would show, his deity of choice was Hercules.

Another attempt to overthrow Commodus probably occurred in 185 when a former soldier named Maternus gathered a small army of deserters and "desperadoes" and plundered the provinces of Gaul and Spain. When a force was sent against them, they broke into small groups, some of which travelled to Rome. The plan was for the outlaws to disguise themselves as praetorian guardsmen during the festival of the goddess Cybele, when costumes were worn by many, and murder the emperor. However, Maternus was betrayed by his own men before he could reach Commodus.

Commodus continued to depend on his father's advisors and gave almost unprecedented power to a series of sometimes corrupt lieutenants, who administered the Empire while he pursued his private interests. The first of these was Saoterus, his chamberlain, who was implicated in Lucilla's plot and killed. He was followed as Commodus' favorite by the praetorian prefect Perennis, who had held the same post under Marcus Aurelius. Perennis was eventually accused of planning to take the throne by his successor, the freedman Cleander, who had risen to become Commodus' new chamberlain. Cleander's power is said to have exceeded even that of Perennis and he grew rich by selling consulships, senatorships, governorships, and other posts for vast sums of money.

Cleander's fall came in 190 when Rome was afflicted by the double misfortune of famine and plague, the latter claiming as many as 2000 lives per day in Rome at its peak. It seems that the food shortage was made worse than necessary by the grain commissioner, a man named Dionysius, who knew that Cleander would take the blame. Indeed, the people rebelled and murdered Cleander, apparently with Commodus' approval.

For the first 10 years of his reign, Commodus had spent most of his time in seclusion at his estates outside of Rome. This may have given rise to rumors about a profligate lifestyle featuring unbridled pleasure-seeking and vast numbers of concubines and pretty boys, violent entertainments, and extravagant feasting. Interestingly, however, the historian Herodian states that when Commodus came to Rome and a more public life in 190 after the fall of Cleander, he "abandoned his interest in moral pursuits", suggesting that Commodus had been involved in more than just fun and games. Also, a life of dissipation up to this time was belied by Commodus' exceptional athletic prowess, as we shall see.

Commodus now began a series of public exhibitions that have made him seem one of the history's most flamboyant and bizarre rulers. His performances in public amphitheaters were of two types: massacres of wild and domesticated animals and gladiatorial combats, the latter always won by the emperor (albeit with wooden sword and shield and no serious bloodshed). Cassius Dio wrote that Commodus appeared in public as a gladiator no fewer than 365 times while Marcus Aurelius was still alive. However, his appearances after 190 were part of a revolutionary program that included dramatic changes in the Emperor's behavior, appearance, and official titles.

Taking advantage of a serious fire in Rome that destroyed the temples of Peace and the goddess Vesta, Commodus "refounded" the city and named it after himself: the "City of Commodus". He renamed the months of the year after his various titles and identified himself so completely with the demigod Hercules that he donned Hercules' lion skin, carried a club in public, and was officially called "Hercules, Son of Jupiter" and "Commodus Hercules".

Commodus acted the part of Hercules in the amphitheater by single-handedly killing vast numbers of wild beasts, including elephants, giraffes, hippos, rhinos, ostriches, and gazelles. He also slaughtered domestic animals, presumably consecrating them for public feasting. His battles with animal foes featured astonishing displays of marksmanship using spears and bow and arrow. For example, he is described as having killed 100 lions with exactly 100 spears – with no misses and each throw being fatal.

The Emperor further imitated the ancient hero by rounding up men who were missing a foot and costuming them as the mythological giants vanquished by Hercules. These giants were said to have had legs like serpents, so Commodus had the men outfitted with prosthetic "serpent legs" and gave them stones made of sponges as weapons to be hurled at him. The historian Dio claims that Commodus clubbed the "giants" to death.

Commodus also publicly adorned himself as the god Mercury, carrying a gilded wand, and wore purple and gold women's robes (apparently in imitation of Hercules' crossdressing phase as the slave of the Lydian queen Omphale). As a gladiator, Commodus wore the outfit of a *secutor*, which consisted of face mask, shield, short sword, and armor for his left, sword-wielding arm.

The Colosseum, the site of many of the emperor's performances, is named for a gigantic statue that once stood nearby. It was between 100 and 120 feet tall and had been erected as a self-portrait by Nero. After Nero's fall, the head was replaced with one of the sun god Sol. Now, Commodus ordered that his own head be substituted, and that a gigantic club and statue of a lion be added to signify his identity as Hercules. An inscription on the base of the statue proclaimed that "Lucius Commodus Hercules, etc., etc." had triumphed over 620 gladiators.

Numerous other statues of Commodus as Hercules were commissioned – including a famous one that survives in the Capitoline Museum in Rome. It shows a bust of the Emperor in his lion skin, carrying a club and holding apples from the garden of the Hesperides, reflecting the 11th of Hercules' famous "12 Labors". Beneath him are two Amazons in supplication, supposedly representing the Emperor's victories over the barbarians. Originally, the statue was flanked by two tritons (male mermaid-like mythological beings). Commodus' intricately curled hair and beard and placid expression create an impression of serenity and benevolence rather than violence. His arms are less heavily muscled than one would expect for Hercules, the strongest of men.

Coins for circulation and medallions for presentation were struck in profusion, showing Commodus in his lion skin with the attributes and appearance of Hercules, the legends proclaiming his new name and titles. A variety of large, artistically engraved medallions of this type were minted at the end of 192 for distribution as New Year gifts.

Commodus was now formally addressed as "the Golden One", "the god", and the Senate voted to call his reign "the Golden Age". The senators were required to call him "lord, the first and most fortunate of men, victorious now and forever".

Needless to say, many Romans were fascinated by this unprecedented imperial behavior. The historian Herodian reports that people from Italy and even the neighboring provinces flocked into the city to witness the spectacle. On one occasion, Commodus apparently performed a drama of his own death and resurrection. Combining stories from Cassius Dio and the *Historia Augusta*, it seems that he ordered the senators to attend the gladiatorial games in equestrian garb and woolen cloaks, as they would wear to a funeral. Commodus, wearing dark clothing, smeared blood from a dead gladiator on his own head and had his helmet carried through the gate of the goddess of funerals (Libitina), as the bodies of dead gladiators were by custom. Though Commodus returned very much alive, Dio claims that the senators took this as a sign that he would pass away in the near future.

It appears that the senators were right, for a plot was soon formed that brought an end to Commodus. According to the historians, the praetorian prefect Laetus, prefect and court chamberlain Eclectus, and Commodus' mistress Marcia decided on the last day of 192 that Commodus had to go. The immediate reason for this action was that the Emperor supposedly planned to murder the two consuls for the coming year and emerge as a gladiator from the gladiatorial barracks on January 1 as their replacement. This was going too far, in the opinion of the conspirators. It was decided that Marcia would poison Commodus' beef (or, alternatively, his wine). However, the emperor vomited up the poison and either threatened his would-be murderers, or quietly prepared a list of people to be executed that included Laetus, Eclectus, and Marcia – as well as most of the leading senators. Alarmed, the conspirators enlisted Narcissus, a young athlete and/or masseur who trained with Commodus, and persuaded him (for a fee) to strangle the Emperor, aged 31, in his bath.

News of the assassination was greeted with dismay by the army and the common people, who adored Commodus, but with celebration by the senators, who detested him. He was replaced by Pertinax, a senator and seasoned soldier who had been consul and a trusted lieutenant of Marcus Aurelius. It is claimed that Pertinax had to be persuaded to accept the throne after Commodus' death, but it seems likely that he had been involved in the conspiracy.

Though the Senate demanded that Commodus' body be dragged by the hook and subjected to every possible indignity, it was secretly buried by Laetus and eventually moved by Pertinax to the Mausoleum of Hadrian. It is ironic that, within two years of his death, Commodus' reputation had been rehabilitated by the new emperor Septimius Severus and he was officially deified. His actions were ratified and he was honored like any other "good" emperor. Dedications to the divine Commodus after his death were made throughout the Empire, especially in the African provinces.

The two most outstanding features of Commodus' reign were his admiration for gladiators and involvement in public gladiatorial contests and the degree of his identification with Hercules. In order to understand him better, it is necessary to gain some insight into their cultural context and meaning.

THE GLADIATORIAL TRADITION

Gladiatorial combats seem to have been introduced by the Etruscans, who ruled Rome until the late 6th century B. C. Initially, they were part of the funerary observances in honor of dead noblemen. As time went on, contests were incorporated into festivals and as entertainment at dinner parties, though they continued to be staged in memory of deceased individuals, sometimes years after their passing. Wealthy and ambitious Romans discovered that sponsoring public contests could be an important way to gain prestige. Julius Caesar won popularity by exhibiting 320 pairs of gladiators in one event while Trajan matched 10,000 men against each other in games that went on for a period of four months.

The custom spread to cities throughout the Empire, as evidenced today by numerous ruined amphitheaters. In some cases, the combatants were condemned criminals or foreign deserters and prisoners of war, but the most popular gladiators formed a class of professional, carefully trained fighters. Many gladiators were slaves – in fact, a common punishment for a slave was to be sold to a troupe of gladiators. However, under the emperors, an increasing number of Romans of free and even noble birth endured social disgrace by enlisting as gladiators in search of excitement, money, and a glorious end. It has been estimated that, by the end of the first-century B. C., more than half of all gladiators were volunteers.

Some Romans, such as Marcus Aurelius and the writer and philosopher Seneca, disapproved of the institution. However, most Romans were fascinated by the gladiators because they provided high drama and excitement while surrendering themselves to the horrors of death. The spectacle was awe-inspiring and entertaining, but also believed to be morally instructive, teaching audiences about courage and honor and hardening them for the challenges of war. It should be remembered that, like most people before the twentieth-century, ancient Romans were accustomed to public executions and punishments and regularly witnessed or participated in the slaughter of animals for food. Hence, they were undoubtedly less squeamish about bloodshed than most people are today.

The extreme popularity of gladiators is beyond question: children imitated them, men argued over their merits, and women adored them. A gladiator's sweat was collected and sold as a prime aphrodisiac and his blood was believed to have curative powers. Women would throw themselves at famous fighters in the streets or bribe guards to give them access to a gladiator's quarters at night.

Unlike Hollywood depictions of them, gladiatorial combats were governed by very specific, almost ritualistic rules of conduct. Winning was not the only thing – losing with grace and courage was also admired and almost always rewarded with a reprieve.

Gladiators were more than entertainers or athletes – they were in a vague but historical sense sacrificial victims, not only to the enjoyment of their masters and the audience, but also to the shades of the dead and, abstractly, to the Roman order of things. The Romans were a profoundly spiritual people who believed that the will of the gods (commonly understood to be different aspects or manifestations of a single divine power) was reflected in external symbols. These included astrological signs, freaks of nature, the entrails of sacrificial animals, and the worldly circumstances of human beings. If a person was conquered by his enemies, or reduced to crime or slavery, it was not because of economic conditions, psychological disorders, or social injustices; it was due to the will of Heaven. Therefore, the miserable condition of a gladiator or criminal was divinely ordained.

The attitude of the gladiators was reflected in their famous salute to Claudius before a mock sea battle: "Hail Emperor; we who are about to die salute you!" Similarly, the *sacramentum gladiatorium*, or gladiators' sacred oath, expressed the fighter's submission. He agreed to allow himself to be "burnt with fire, shackled with chains, whipped with rods, and killed with steel." The gladiator surrendered himself utterly to his master, dedicating his body and soul to him. Some measure of salvation was believed to come from meeting one's destiny with dignity and aplomb. The gladiator's oath made him a co-conspirator in his own destruction. He renounced both fear and hope and welcomed death, which made him in a sense unconquerable. If the crowd and one's betters were entertained or inspired by a noble struggle and a valiant death, so much the better; the gladiator had transformed his degradation into glory.

THE MEANING OF HERCULES

In the Greco-Roman world and beyond, Hercules was a beloved symbol of human potential. He was believed to have been a historical figure who lived before the Trojan War, or about 1500 years before Commodus was born. The son of Jupiter (in the Greek pantheon Heracles, the son of Zeus) and of the mortal woman Alcmene, he was the first man to become a god as a reward for his courage and exceptional services to humanity.

Hercules' achievements began early when he strangled a pair of serpents sent by the goddess Hera to kill him. This was the first of many extraordinary feats of strength and ingenuity attributed to Hercules, the most famous of which are known as "The Twelve Labors". In one tale, he journeyed to the Underworld and rescued the princess Alcestis, thus defeating Death. The stories of Hercules – and the numerous cults, shrines, and temples dedicated to him – ensured that he remained a potent presence in the minds and hearts of the Greeks and Romans.

Hercules was, in a sense, the Greco-Roman equivalent of Jesus Christ in that he was believed to have died and been reborn. Hercules' death came when his wife mistakenly poisoned him by giving him a cloak soaked with the poisonous blood of the Hydra, whom her husband had killed. When Hercules donned the cloak, it welded itself to his flesh and began to dissolve it away. Unable to remove the cloak and aware that his end had come, Hercules climbed onto a funeral pyre, where his body was burned while his soul was taken into Heaven by the gods.

This was a death of the body only as his spirit continued to live among the gods for eternity as one of them. He had demonstrated how a man should live in order to be granted immortality. Therefore, to live in imitation of Hercules was a spiritual path. People prayed and sacrificed to Hercules in the hopes that he would aid them in their troubles and help them conquer death. When Jesus became the central figure on Roman sarcophagi as the principal hope of the departed, it was Hercules that he replaced.

Because he had been rewarded by the gods for his worldly achievements with deification, Hercules became a sort of "alter-ego" for many ancient leaders. Among these were Alexander the Great, who, like Commodus, was portrayed wearing the lion skin, and Mark Antony, the lover of Cleopatra and rival of the first Roman emperor Augustus. After Commodus, both the 3rd Century usurper Postumus and emperor Maximian identified themselves with Hercules, the latter also wearing the lion skin in official portraits.

The late historian Michael Grant wrote that emperors modeled themselves on the aspect of Hercules that best suited their capabilities and tastes. He said that to Trajan the warrior, Hercules was the conqueror of the world. To Hadrian, he was the great traveler. To Antoninus Pius, he was the redeemer who struggled for Italy against its legendary monsters. For Marcus Aurelius, Hercules was "the hero of self-sacrifice and love of humanity: the martyr to duty". But for Commodus, Hercules was "the mythical symbol of his rule".

Commodus presented himself variously as Hercules the victorious, the founder and protector of Rome, the conqueror of the giants, the androgynous, health-giving servant of Omphale, and the killer of beasts and monsters.

There were similarities in the lives of Hercules and Commodus that the latter would not have missed. Both were twins, precocious youths of royal blood, and initiates of the Eleusinian Mysteries. Many of the performances and acquired skills of the young emperor were designed to enhance the resemblance. In the end, both died at the hands of others in the prime of life.

THE CORRESPONDENCE

(Imagined)

NERVA TO TRAJAN

My esteemed son and colleague,

Greetings! I hope that the northern winter is not too harsh and your new duties as Caesar not too onerous.

During our brief time together in October for the adoption ceremony, I came to realize even more powerfully the wisdom of my choice of heir and successor. I also began to develop a genuine affection for you. Though you are not my son by blood, the gods have connected us in a way that is just as binding and, perhaps, even more important. Therefore, I feel that it is my duty to instruct you as a son – to share my thoughts of how I have failed and how you might succeed, both as a man and as an emperor. I do this for your welfare, for my welfare, and for the good of Rome.

Our paths to the principate have been very different. You have been chosen because of your abilities and achievements as a general and administrator - as a leader of men. I was chosen because I survived; because I maintained political prominence during dangerous times without offending anyone. In a lifetime of 68 years, I have achieved very little – I have won no battles, governed no provinces, built no monuments, nor distinguished myself in any profession. Nevertheless, I was shrewd and flexible enough to befriend and influence emperors like Nero and Domitian without taking on their stamp or sharing in their infamy and destruction.

I have only been an emperor for a year and three months – and my reign has been unsteady. It would certainly have ended months ago had I not associated myself with you as my colleague and heir. You may hesitate to take advice from one so weak and ineffectual. But I have some observations about being an emperor that you should at least take into consideration.

Don't stop being a general. I had no influence with the army, so I tried to muster support by catering to everyone else. I lowered provincial tribute, gave sixty million sesterces worth of land to the poor, cancelled inheritance taxes, repaired roads and aqueducts, expanded the Circus Maximus while adding new games and races, pampered and flattered the senators, recalled exiles, loaned money to landowners, and gave away or auctioned off my possessions to forestall envy and pay for my benefactions. However, despite all this, it is only your influence with the army that keeps me on the throne. Be an emperor and remain conscious of the welfare of all your subjects, but don't try to please everyone – and keep your army boots on!

Be fearless – and make sure that everyone knows you are fearless. When the praetorians stormed the palace and demanded that I turn over the men responsible for Domitian's murder, I was defiant. They manhandled me and placed me under arrest, but I did not flinch; I exposed my bare neck to them and dared them to strike. They did not. When Crassus and his men conspired to overthrow me, I learned of their plot and armed them with swords - to show that I knew their intentions and was not afraid. They were ashamed and confessed. Had I shown fear in either case, I would have been slaughtered. I was spared because they knew that a brave man is never vengeful.

Don't let your portrait artists show your age and imperfections. The common people want to think that you are godlike in form as well as in wisdom, so see to it that you are beautiful on all your coins and statues. I was persuaded to allow my countenance to be shown accurately – as a return to the tough-minded realism of our Republican past. It seemed a healthy response to Domitian's vanity. However, no one fears a feeble-looking Caesar. Augustus knew best, and you can never go wrong by following his lead: have yourself portrayed as young and beautiful for as long as you live, no matter what the truth may become.

I also have some observations about being a human being that you may value, as they come from one who has lived longer and wandered further from the course of virtue than you have. I see few flaws in you, but there is one that we share – an excessive love of wine. When we are young, this makes us seem accessible, agreeable, and reassuringly human. When we are old, it makes us seem demented, irascible, and physically and emotionally unstable. In my youth, I followed Nero in swallowing vast amounts of food and wine - and regurgitating so I could do it all again. Now I vomit involuntarily. A legion of imperial cooks prepares delicacies I cannot digest and serves wine I cannot keep down. Be moderate, or be sorry.

As I look back on my life, I can see that the reasons I succeeded in politics are the same reasons that I have failed as a human being. I rose to prominence because I was agreeable, expedient, flexible – I went with the flow of things. I always took the path of moderation and flattery, always adjusting my views and behavior when change was in the air. Had I been devoted to my principles and guided by my conscience, I would have died long ago - but I would have died a man of honor rather than a mere footnote in the history of other men's lives. I succeeded and survived because I was clever – but I produced nothing. I was occasionally useful, that is all. You are capable and active, an initiator. I survived by my wits – it is better to survive by your deeds.

I ask that, when your life begins to fade, you will write a similar letter to your successor. I pray to the gods that you will have that opportunity. If such letters become customary, and if each succeeding emperor takes them to heart, then perhaps each will be a better ruler and better man than his predecessor and the entire world will benefit.

With pious prayers for your long and successful life,

Marcus Cocceius Nerva Caesar Augustus (Nerva)

TRAJAN TO HADRIAN

My dear Publius,

With this letter, I send you a diamond that was given to me by my adopted father Nerva. He believed that it conferred mystical power and good fortune on its owner, so he gave it to me when I became his successor.

Yes, your surmise is correct – you shall be my heir. If you ever doubted it, consider that no one else is as prepared for the role - by experience, station, or family connection. I will arrange your adoption shortly and notify the senate in Rome. I have delayed in this for many reasons, but, if I am honest with myself, it was because I intended to live at least as long as Augustus (75 years). That would have given me another dozen years – too long to have a colleague who might become the focus of plots to put me out of the way. But now I am partially paralyzed, suffering from edema, and, it seems, abandoned by the gods, so I must make arrangements for the future.

After Nerva adopted me, he wrote me a letter of advice, which I also send to you now, enumerating his principles for wise rule and confessing shortcomings that he hoped I could avoid. He asked me to follow his lead by writing a frank letter to my successor when the time came. The time has come. If I had written to you just one or two years ago, my advice would have been very different than it will be now.

Some of Nerva's advice was useful and I am glad that I took it, so I pass it on to you. For example, he warned me to control my drinking. I took this to heart and have always instructed my servants to refuse to serve me when I call for more wine than I should. Therefore, I have never been intoxicated in public as emperor.

He also advised me to appear fearless, whether I was or not. He said that this was the best way to scare off plots. Accordingly, when I first presented my praetorian prefect with his sword, I invited him to use it for me if I ruled well - and against me if I ruled badly. When there were rumors that Licinius Sura was plotting to overthrow me, I went to his house unguarded and submitted to a bath, shave, meal – and even had my eyes anointed by his servant – to show that I was not afraid and could not be intimidated by rumor. The fact that I have always been accessible to my subjects, mingling with them freely and walking through the streets of Rome as a private citizen, shows that courage is rewarded. (Of course, my bodyguard was always nearby, just in case.)

Nerva also advised me to stay close to the army and keep it busy – that there is no holding on to power without military support. I have certainly kept it busy, with two major wars in Dacia and one in the East. I have even invented threats when necessary to justify maneuvers and general readiness among the troops. You will have a greater challenge – to keep the army ready and busy without warfare for, as my military adventures have clearly shown, there are no lands outside the Empire that we should covet. Give the men useful work to do – building bridges and fortifying boundaries - and drill them constantly, but only go to war if you must and only for defense.

I have been called *Optimus Princeps* – the best of princes. I was praised for my benefactions to the people - building roads, bridges, baths, and other public structures - and for keeping the Empire safe and prosperous. My victories in Dacia, the annexation of Arabia, the conquest of Armenia, Adiabene, Mesopotamia, the subjugation of Parthia – all seemed to confirm my abilities and the favor of the gods. But recent events have shaken my confidence to the ground and have made me reconsider my whole career – even the way that I have lived my life.

Some believe that the gods send us warnings and signs of their displeasure. If so, what should I conclude from the catastrophes that have followed in my wake the past two years? The earthquake in Antioch – tens of thousands killed and the third city of the Empire reduced to rubble and dust. I myself barely survived, forced to squirm through a window to escape my building. I saw bloodshed and mutilation that far exceeded any battle or barbarian atrocity.

However, I ignored the thundering voice of Providence and continued my eastern campaign. Meanwhile, the Jews revolted in Cyrene, in Cyprus, in Egypt – their devastation even surpassing that of the earthquake. This took me completely by surprise. I had not grasped the depth of resentment over the Jewish tax, the destruction of their temple in Jerusalem almost half a century ago, or their loyalty and economic ties to Parthia, where many Jews live today. Only the barbarity of their uprising – the flaying and dismemberment and murder of half a million Greek and Roman victims – showed me the depth of feelings that I should have perceived.

And then, when I boasted that I had eclipsed even Alexander in my conquests, my new eastern vassals rose up and expelled my garrisons, threatening to cut off my lines of supply. I was forced to compromise, to recognize rulers not of my choosing. Even the Dacian king Decebalus had not prepared me for the duplicity and deception I encountered in that part of the world. Worse still was the disgrace of Hatra: having to leave that desert fortress unconquered; withdrawing my sick and humbled troops before they died of thirst.

And then, as you know, my body rebelled against me. A stroke left me paralyzed and swelling with fluid. Now I am prostrate and at the mercy of doctors, on my way back to Rome, so weak that my wife Plotina must write this letter for me. My once mighty hand can't even hold a pen, much less a sword.

What am I to learn from all of this – what wisdom shall I pass on to you?

While lying in my sickbed, I have had the opportunity to review my life, to ponder what I might have done differently – what you might want to do differently. I find that you have already done much of it, often without my approval. I apologize for that. We have often quarreled about lifestyle, hairstyles – trivial stuff. I can see now that I am out of date, trying to be Julius Caesar as I imagined him. You are the future – a cosmopolitan man with sophisticated tastes and an open mind. A man of the world and not just a Roman in the narrow, old-fashioned sense.

It is no longer enough to be a man of action, or skilled only in the arts of politics, economics, and war; an emperor must also be a man of ideas, capable of understanding the disparate cultures that make up the Roman world. As you know, I am not an educated man. I have little interest in art, music, poetry, rhetoric, philosophy – the so-called finer things. However, I now believe that a balanced and cultivated mind is necessary for a balanced rule. Develop all aspects of yourself – remember that your personal growth and fulfillment will benefit the Empire. What is good for you is good for everyone because the more you know, the more you will understand.

I travelled through most of the world – but I saw very little of it. What I saw were forts and bridges, potentates and soldiers – everywhere, the same soldiers. I love them, but they look to me for meaning and I look to them for meaning. In the end, we followed each other to Hatra, where neither strength nor courage could win the day. So it is with armies and empires in the end.

You should travel even more than I have done, but with open eyes and ears, so that you will know all of your people. It was because I didn't understand the Jews and the oriental states that they surprised and ruined me. Endeavour to learn about the ways of all peoples so that you can rule from a position of understanding rather than power alone.

Nerva was shrewd; I have been active – we both survived a very dangerous job, which has proved fatal to most of our predecessors. But if you wish to improve on our reigns, then you must add knowledge to cleverness and achievement. If you succeed, then your rule will be informed and you will be less likely to face death in misery and failure as I do now.

It is a monumental task that I bequeath to you, my cousin, but you have the qualities that are needed to succeed - to surpass all who have come before you. The gods grant that you will.

Marcus Ulpius Nerva Traianus Augustus (Trajan)

Hadrian to Antoninus Pius

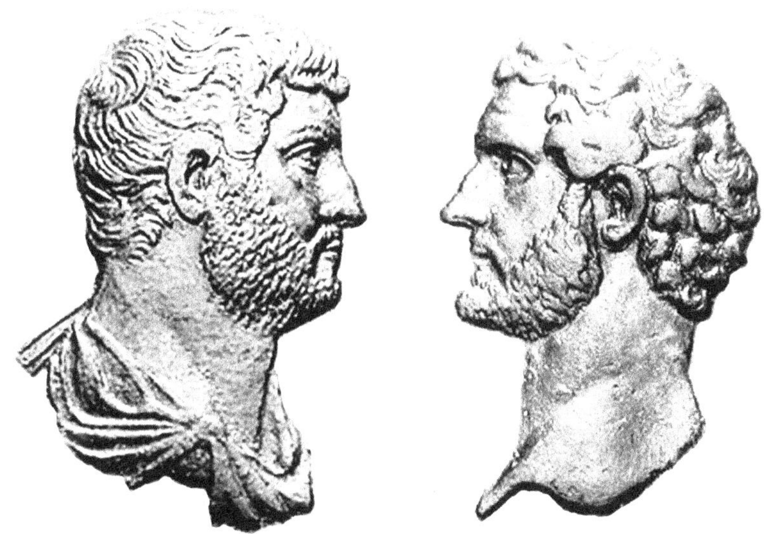

My dear Antoninus,

This letter is also for young Marcus Aurelius – please pass it on to him when the time is right. In truth, it is more for him than for you, as you are only 10 years my junior and already set in your excellent ways.

When my deified father Trajan was facing death, he wrote to advise me how I might improve on his rule and on his life. He was following the injunction of Nerva, who had done the same and had requested that this become a tradition for succeeding emperors.

Now, I considered Trajan to be a fine general and statesman, but I had little respect for his intellect – and I knew that he had little respect for my lifestyle and academic pursuits. So I was surprised that he urged me to educate myself; to improve my mind in areas not directly related to government. You know that I needed no encouragement in this. From my boyhood, I was determined to understand our Empire and its workings so completely that, if I was the only Roman in an empty land, I could reconstruct our world in all of its variety and grandeur from my own skill and knowledge.

As I have often said to the annoyance of others – there is no one who knows more or has seen more or can do more than I. Modesty aside, I am the most brilliant and most accomplished man of my time. My understanding of military arts and sciences is unsurpassed. I am a gifted poet, sculptor, painter, and musician, innovative architect, accomplished mathematician, master astrologer, and I was, in my prime, an unparalleled hunter, mountain-climber, athlete, connoisseur of art, and gourmand.

I felt that it was my duty to be all these things – because the gods gave me the ability and opportunity and because I believed that this would make me the best of rulers. We called Trajan *Optimus Princeps* – "the best of princes". The only way I could surpass him, as it is every son's duty to do, was to be the best in everything – not just ruling the Empire. In order to do this, I had to know everything and see everything. I thought that comprehensive knowledge of the world would bring success, happiness, and wisdom.

I am proud of many accomplishments – of recognizing and addressing countless needs in the provinces, of defining and strengthening our borders, of establishing peace and refraining from unnecessary expansion. I came to know the people of the Empire in all their languages, religions, and customs. I was tireless in my service to my subjects and I believe that I did much good for the people under my power.

As no emperor worked harder or travelled more widely than I did, I felt justified in indulging my desire for excellence – in my surroundings, my bedfellows, my food, wine, and entertainment. I built the villa in Tibur, decorated it with the finest art and architecture, and made it an earthly paradise. I lived like a god because I could – and because I believed that my mind had elevated me above the normal run of men. I believed that we approach the divine condition through our intellect, and my intellect was the greatest of all.

And what have my achievements and self-indulgences done for me? Have they made me *Optimus Princeps*? Would I recommend a similar path for you and for Marcus?

I would not. Now I am an old man, perhaps before my time - worn out by my exertions, by my excesses. My senses are exhausted, incapable of enjoyment. I am despised by many because of my arrogant, competitive nature. I had to be the best at everything – so everyone else was forced to dissemble or under-achieve because they feared my envy. Some even felt compelled to modify the truth rather than let me be wrong. My attainments, great as they were, have been eroded by time and infirmity – there is always something new to learn or something old that I am forgetting. I am no longer the best at anything, but I dare not admit it because my position and my power are built on the pretense than I am infallible.

Because I wallowed in facts and sense pleasures, my mind and my senses are worn out. It was my intention to spend my final days at my villa at Tibur, dedicating myself to poetry, music, and literature. Instead, I writhe in agony, preoccupied by the mundane concerns of the body. For all my study, I haven't learned how to face death, which means I haven't learned how to face life. There has been expansiveness in my learning, but not depth. It is better to know one thing, one person, one place completely than to have a passing knowledge about everything. The more I learned, the farther I travelled, the less I knew. It seems a paradox, but it is true. There are no roots to hold me in place when the winds of time are blowing.

When I look at you, Antoninus, I see a man beloved by his family, by his servants, by his friends. I see a man whose virtues win respect and affection rather than awe. You are unpretentious, amiable, patient, thrifty, forgiving – all the things that I am not. These qualities have brought you peace and the love of your fellows - far better than what I have received. Marcus would do better to follow your lead than to follow mine. Knowledge without virtue is empty.

My advice to you and to Marcus is this: cultivate virtue above worldly knowledge. Learn to recognize the best men and let them be the experts – your eyes and ears and minds. Don't exhaust yourself with travel - stay at home with your family as much as you can. Seek contentment – this is a far greater gift to share with the Empire than sophistication. Be modest and unassuming; it is not fair for an emperor to compete with his subjects. If you take my advice, you will be more popular than I have been. The people will support and imitate an emperor they like, but not one they fear or before whom they stand in awe.

Augustus understood that Rome is built on families – and that the imperial family should be the model for all. Trajan understood this as well. I have failed in this. Having no children, and having little in common with my wife Sabina, I put my friendships first. You would be wiser to emphasize your ties to wife, children, and grandchildren. These are the bonds that your subjects know and share, that hold things together. Advertise these bonds – exaggerate your domestic tranquility, if necessary. You must be the exemplary Roman family man – the standard of virtue and stability. That is what is called for in these times of prosperity and peace. That will do more than laws or victories to set an example for society and uplift the moral character of the people.

May you have fewer regrets than I do when you pass the scepter to Marcus, the hope and future of mankind.

Traianus Hadrianus Augustus (Hadrian)

ANTONINUS PIUS TO MARCUS AURELIUS

Marcus,

You already know about the enclosed letters, written by each dying emperor to his successor. I have been reviewing them and have been struck by how each emperor anticipated the advice from his predecessor. Nerva warned Trajan to be more active and involved with the army – which he already was. Trajan told Hadrian to seek knowledge – which Hadrian was already doing. Hadrian advised me to stay close to Rome and family, which I had already chosen. And now, it is my turn to advise you – and, again, my advice has been anticipated.

You have already learned what it takes to rule – you are already as fine a man as I have ever known. I will not take up your time with platitudes or practical advice. The only gifts I can give you now are my regrets - that you may learn from them and surpass me even further than you have already done.

My greatest regret – which dominates my thoughts – is that you may inherit an Empire on the verge of war. King Vologases in Parthia seems bent on hostilities, and there are ominous reports of unrest beyond our northern frontier. The German tribes have learned to fight like Romans, and you will probably find them difficult to subdue. I fear that I have been tardy in perceiving and preparing for these threats – perhaps I focused too much on affairs in Rome and Italy and relied too much on my advisors to keep abreast of conditions in the provinces.

But as much as I worry about the future, I know that you are aware of the risks, and know that crises are inevitable in the ebb and flow of history. No border or alliance survives forever – we must continually adjust, knowing that, in the end, all empires become dust. There are more important issues for a man to consider - even an emperor.

Trajan once said that he tried to be the sort of Caesar he had wished to serve before he came to the throne. I took this to heart and tried to have the qualities I had wanted in a ruler – accessibility, devotion to duty, humility. But what we want others to be is not always what is good for them, or for ourselves.

For the sake of duty, I controlled my selfish passions – but to such an extent that they were extinguished. I neglected personal growth for the sake of service. I have been too much the slave of duty and proper behavior, of polite rectitude. My advice to you is this: do not neglect your inner life for the sake of responsibilities that can be handled by others.

After the loss of my beloved wife Faustina, I immersed myself in my work to escape my grief. I excused my overwork as my duty, but I can see now that I was hiding from my own pain. For the uplifting of my soul, I relied too much on outer religious practice. I was always meticulous and regular in both my public and private worship, believing that piety was sufficient. Now I know that piety and proper behavior are not enough. I am facing death and find that I am unready. There is no peace or resignation - worship and hard work have brought me no closer to understanding.

You must be active in your own salvation, Marcus! You must strive tirelessly for wisdom and self-knowledge if you are to face death without fear. Yes, you must also be outwardly religious, for you are the model of others and devotional practice benefit the common sort. But do not rely on religious observance and ethical behavior to bring you peace.

Others may think that I am serene and wise, but, without the love and support of my family, I would be lost. My life would lack meaning, and meaning based on the feelings and actions of others is hollow; dependent on outer circumstances that are subject to change.

I am not saying that my life has been a failure. I believe that I have done much good and have been an adequate ruler, for the most part. My people have shown their love and appreciation for me – but their praise does nothing for me now, and I cannot take it to the grave. I have learned how to live – but not how to die. You must do better – continue your journey into yourself and find the philosophical muscle you will need to meet both death and adversity with true equanimity. I know that this is already your goal – pursue it in every thought and deed. Do not let ruling the Roman Empire keep you from becoming a complete man, Marcus. Remember, it is not enough to be pious; you must also be wise.

With fatherly affection,

Titus (Antoninus Pius)

Marcus Aurelius to Commodus

My dear son,

Junius Rusticus taught me to avoid fine writing and compose letters that are simple and direct (*Meditations*, 1, 7). This letter will probably be even more blunt than usual - but remember that it is inspired by the warmest affection and love.

You have seen the letters written by each of my predecessors. These offered advice for sound rule and personal development. They also confessed mistakes in the hope they would not be repeated. My intentions are similar - but Lucius, none of these men wrote as a father, as I do. They wrote with varying degrees of affection, but their first concern was for the Empire; to educate the new Caesar and guide him in his conduct as a ruler. No doubt, you expect me to do the same, extolling the virtues of industry, attention to duty, respect for propriety, sobriety, loyalty, blah, blah, blah - so that you may become a just and capable ruler. As you will see, I have a different objective in mind –

but I believe that the result will be the same.

I came to the throne intending to be a man of peace, presiding over an age of prosperity and general well-being. I saw myself as a benevolent caretaker and gentle reformer, occupied with improving the system of justice and preserving the conditions bequeathed to me by Antoninus and his predecessors. Instead, my reign has seen war, plague, invasion, famine; suffering unmatched since the days of Hannibal. The world that I pass on to you is quite different from the one I inherited, and you will have to be a very different sort of emperor than I have been in order to rule it properly. I believe that you were born for this task and that nature has suited you for it.

As we have agreed, you should abandon the attempt to expand our northern borders after I have died. If I should withdraw now, it would be seen as a failure - but your accession as sole ruler will present an opportunity for a change of policy without loss of face. The campaign has not been a failure; the northern frontier is now secure, and it should remain so for many years to come. But the army is exhausted and our resources will not support continuing this war.

If you regret the loss of opportunities to be victorious in battle, remember that there is no essential difference between a spider's conquest of a fly and a Caesar's conquest of a people. These are petty, unnecessary victories that may distract you from the greater campaign - the pursuit of truth. (X, 10) Caesars are like smoke: gone in an instant. Don't let being a Caesar interfere with being a real human being. (X, 31)

After you have inspected the frontier, you should return to Rome. I have been away from the capital too much in recent years. The people there have grown restless without an emperor to dote upon. They look for other leaders and heroes, which is dangerous.

Perhaps the growth in the number of Christians in the capital is because of this. They claim that the Nazarene is the only son of god and the king of men. They pretend that man and nature are separate from the divine and deny the existence of gods other than their own; they reject the idea that the emperor is Jupiter's representative on earth. They preach peace at any cost and refuse to do their part in defending the Empire from its enemies. These ideas are threats to the security of the state and to imperial authority and this cult should continue to be suppressed. Stay in Rome as much as possible to support the state religion and be the focus of the people's veneration, for they must venerate someone.

During my years on the front, many friends tried to console me for my difficulties – for the hardships of warfare and life in a military camp, far from the comforts of Rome. It is a great irony that these circumstances were a blessing to me, for the wars required me to be away from the distractions of the court and gave me the opportunity to explore myself, to turn within and pursue philosophy. On the frontier, I was able to live simply – to be myself more than ever before. I hope that you, too, will be able to avoid the life of the court, Lucius, to find solace so that you can tend to your own development as a person.

What I have learned through thought, study, and self-examination I hope to pass on to you now, for my duty to you as a human being and as my son is paramount. My first concern is your welfare as a man, dear Lucius - your personal happiness and fulfillment. I believe that what is good for the individual is also good for society, and what is best for a man is to live in accordance with his highest nature. (V, 8; XI, 13)

Don't be distracted by your power and glory. The best way for you to become the perfect emperor is for you to become the perfect human being. This will require courage and determination – and a refusal to be deterred from your objective. Look on your role as Caesar as your stepmother and your quest for truth your real mother. Do your duty to your stepmother, but honor your real mother above all! (VI, 12) Discover what your nature requires, accept it and pursue it with your whole being. Don't bother with anything else. (X, 2)

Don't be concerned about praise or blame from others – most people aren't even satisfied with themselves. (III, 5) Don't bother about other people's opinions about how you should live – follow your own nature and remain focused on where you are going. (VII, 55) Remember, it is possible to be a divine man without anyone noticing. (VII, 67) Don't worry how you seem to others ; happiness can only be found by following your true nature. (VIII, 1)

Try not to pray for anything – if you must pray, then ask to be released from desire for anything. (IX, 40) Material things are constantly changing and cannot touch the soul. (IV, 3) Never mistake your body for who you are. Your body is just a tool, like an axe or a pencil, to be used by your spirit. (X, 38) Realize that time is short, my son. Only the present moment exists – the past is gone and the future uncertain. (III, 10) Clear away the clouds from your mind and know who you are before your life ends. Perform every action as if it is your last – never postpone self-inquiry. (II, 4)

Remember that you can choose to live with a calm and peaceful mind, even if the entire world cries out against you and wild beasts tear you limb from limb. (VII, 68) No one can hurt you unless you allow them to. (II, 1) Be like a sea cliff that remains steadfast against the thundering waves. (IV, 51) You are in control of your mind, which is part of the divine and therefore omnipotent. (II, 1) It has the power to become whatever it wants. (XI, 1)

If you can become a good man, a man of virtue and equanimity, then you will enter into a new life. Such a man has put off the body and devotes himself to acting without attachment or expectation, leaving the fruits to nature. (X, 11, 14) He cares nothing for the opinions of others; he cares only for following God. Remember that the gods wish for all beings to be like them. (X, 8)

God sees the divine in each one of us – you should do the same. (XII, 2) Purify your vision and you will see that the universe is calm and stable, ever-young and perfect. (XII, 22) Then you will be godlike, following God's path. (XII, 23) Your soul is God and of God. (XII, 26) Respect the divinity within you and you will be a man worthy of the universe that produced you. You will no longer be a stranger in your own land. (XII, 1) As there is one light from the sun, there is one soul, distributed among infinite natures and individuals, but still one. (XII, 32)

Always be mindful of the divine spark within you – and worship it sincerely as the presence of God. (II, 13) Remember that you are connected to the divine – you can't do anything without divine inspiration and support. (III, 13) Your mind will take on the character of what you think about habitually. Therefore, always think of the highest. (V, 16) Your reasoning mind is a piece of God, given by Him to guide you. (V, 27)

Always perceive the universe as one living being, with one substance and one soul. (IV, 40) Everything is connected and pervaded by one divinity. (VII, 9) Retire into your own soul with your whole being and as often as possible – you will be renewed and find peace. (IV, 3) Focus on the source of all. (VI, 36) Your mind will be cleansed and you will return to your work invigorated and contented. (IV, 3) Go deep within. You will find goodness inside yourself and, as long as you keep digging, joy will continue to bubble up. (VII, 59)

You injure your soul when you play a part; when you say something that you do not believe. You must be true to yourself. (II, 16) No one can keep you from living in accord with your own nature. (VI, 58) Let men see a real human being who lives according to divine nature. If they cannot endure it, let them kill you. That is better than to live as the common man lives. (X, 15) The noblest ambition that any man can have is to imitate the gods. (per Julian, *The Caesars*, 333)

Remember that you are the rising sun, as I am the setting sun. May your reign be the dawn of a new age!

Your father, Marcus Aurelius

Commodus to Divus Marcus Aurelius

To my divine father among the gods,

Do you realize what a lonely man you have made me? You gave me a vision, an obsession shared by few and pursed by none of my acquaintance. And yet I do not blame you, Father, for I have taken your words to heart and they have brought me joys beyond description.

I have lived according to your principles - that what is best for my soul is what is best for all men, that I must be true to my nature and become my highest self, whatever the cost or consequences. I have made the imitation of the gods my sole objective.

As you intended, I have entrusted the running of the Empire to the older, wiser men you left to advise me. I stayed away from Rome and pursued wisdom and discipline privately in the belief that this was the best service I could give mankind. Perhaps some of those who ruled for me became corrupt in my absence. This is a small matter – the transfer of wealth from one group of men to another is of no consequence in the larger scheme of things. And the fruits of my practices, which I can now share with all mankind, have been worth the price.

In the beginning, I asked myself, how may I imitate the gods – which should I model myself after? I considered my position in life, my natural inclinations, my abilities, the desires of my heart, and my deity appeared to me in visionary splendor: Hercules - the first man to become a god, the ideal ruler and benefactor of mankind, the enemy of evil and master of time!

You taught me that a man cannot command until he has learned to obey (*Meditations*, XI, 29), so I surrendered myself to Hercules. I became his disciple in all things, disciplining my body and my mind to become like his. I meditated on his form and affirmed my oneness with him with every thought and every breath. I strengthened my limbs and practiced the arts of hunting and fighting until I became like him - the greatest marksman in the world. It was Hercules who aimed my bow and threw my javelin.

At times I felt lost - a failure and a charlatan; an Icarus soaring too near the sun. But I kept striving. I knew that I could not allow myself to be less than you were, and that if I failed to surpass you, then I would have failed both of us. You took me to the verge of Heaven, Father, but I had to make the leap. It took me ten years to become ready. Whenever I wavered, I remembered your words: what pulls the strings is that which is hidden within. (X, 38)

And then the glorious moment came. I felt my arms become his arms, my chest become his chest, my mind become his mind, my heart become his heart. My head filled with light and I was suffused with a power and joy and understanding that I had never imagined possible. Every hair and pore tingled with his presence. My true nature was revealed and I became a god; a true human being!

When I was firm in my identification, I wondered how I might bring this light into the world. I remembered our experiences at Eleusis – how we saw ourselves as human and divine, male and female, mortal and immortal. How can a man live as a mere man after those experiences? I remembered that these truths are open to all and realized that I was born to be a model and example – to reveal my divinity to the whole world. Surely, this is what is meant by leadership; this is why I was born into such a high position.

I wondered how I should reveal my divine nature. I considered the Christians, whose numbers have doubled during my lifetime. My mistress Marcia, who is knowledgeable of their ways and beliefs, made me appreciate the power and persuasiveness of their cult. She showed me why a human intercessor has such great appeal to the people – a divine man who can bring God's grace into the hearts of men.

Marcia told me that the Christians look to the apotheosis of their Christ for their own redemption. I realized that if I can serve this role for my people, by following Hercules' path to immortality, then I can become the perfect prince. I would not be a feeble savior, like their Christ, who was tortured and executed by a minor official in a minor province. How much greater would be my example and service to mankind!

And so I gave myself to the Fates. I abandoned all pretense that I was Lucius, son of Marcus, mortal king in a temporary world. I am Commodus Hercules, the immortal savior! I donned the lion skin, I took up the club. I presented myself in the arena as Hercules reborn, the master of beasts and enemies, the unconquerable protector sent by God to preserve and renew the world!

When Rome was beset by plague, I became Hercules Omphale, the giver of health. When the Temple of Peace and Vesta were destroyed by fire, I became Hercules Romanus Conditor, the re-founder of Rome, which I renamed the City of Commodus to proclaim my mission and the dawn of a New Age. When famine struck, I slaughtered the animals in the arena and provided meat. None of this was done by "Lucius" – it was done by Hercules in the body of Lucius.

But the body of Lucius is frail and temporary. I considered the majesty of Hercules after his death and ascension to the Heaven. How much more powerful he became, able to answer the prayers of the entire world rather than just one city or one king! I came to understand that the imitation of the gods must not be halfhearted; a masquerade that ends when the dinner party is over. It must be genuine and complete – we must be willing to give up everything, including our very lives.

As you must know, I have been miraculously saved from plots on several occasions. When Lucilla sent young Quintianus against me, the gods slowed his tongue and addled his mind so that my guards could apprehend him before he struck. And then the Mother of the Gods saved me from the renegade Maternus by changing the hearts of his men and causing them to deliver him up. When Perennis and Cleander coveted the throne, they were exposed and eliminated without my having to raise a finger.

I believe that the gods intervened – perhaps you among them - so that I could prepare for my apotheosis. The time has finally come. I have revealed my true identity on coins and statues, in my dress and demeanor, in my names and titles. I duplicated the feats of Hercules in the arena, vanquishing monsters and beasts and hosts of gladiators – symbols of the evils that threaten the Empire. Then I gave the people a foreshadowing of my death – the death of my body, that is. I smeared myself with blood and had them carry my armor through the Gate of Libitina. Tomorrow, on New Year's Day, I will follow Hercules onto the funeral pyre in the Flavian Amphitheater. I will burn this body to ashes so that I may take my place in Heaven.

If the archaic Greek Hercules, hero of a small and primitive people, became so great after he became a god, what will become of an emperor of Rome? I must have the courage to find out, Father! I am limited by this body. When I leave it, my powers will be endless. I will serve the world with omniscience, omnipotence, and infinite grace. Surely this is worth the sacrifice of a few small bones and particles of flesh that will pass away soon in any case?

Of course, there are many who think I am mad – how many more there may be when I have left my body! But you were right – I cannot let praise or blame keep me from my destiny. What do the senators know of my inner state?

They may wonder who will rule the Empire when I am gone? Does it matter? Perhaps Pompeianus, perhaps Pertinax. In truth, it is always the gods who rule. Nothing moves or happens without their permission – without *our* permission. Father, the time has come for us to be reunited on the throne of Heaven!

Your son and disciple, Commodus Hercules

EPILOGUE

(Imagined)

Pertinax had difficulty hiding his surprise and disdain as Marcia, Laetus, and Eclectus were ushered into the *triclinium* of his home in Rome. Pertinax disapproved of Marcia, believing that she was unworthy of the position and confidences that Commodus had bestowed upon her. Nevertheless, it was Marcia who spoke first.

"The emperor plans to kill himself at the New Year's celebration in the amphitheater tomorrow."

She paused for the news to sink in. Pertinax said nothing.

Laetus continued: "He plans to lead the gladiators out of their barracks in procession into the arena – himself in the forefront in his secutorial armor. Once there, he will engage in mock combat with each of them in turn. They will pretend to defend themselves and then offer their throats in supplication. Commodus will spare them and have an attendant present them with coin and insignias of their freedom."

Eclectus picked up the story. "Then a lion will be released into the arena, which Commodus will kill with a spear. He will flay the dead animal and don its bleeding skin. He will pretend that the blood is poisoned and, like Hercules in his cloak, he will suffer and pretend to be unable to remove it."

Marcia: "Then he will climb onto a towering wooden pyre, which has already been prepared, and will be burned alive by the gladiators as a sacrifice to the gods. Commodus believes that he will be taken into Heaven, just as Hercules was, and that he will return with divine powers to inaugurate a Golden Age, free from want and disease."

Pertinax tugged at his long beard. "This is madness, nothing but madness. It cannot happen."

Laetus replied, "We cannot stop him; it is a matter of faith."

Pertinax bellowed: "We *must* stop him. If he cannot be dissuaded, then he must be removed. Order will not survive a spectacle such as this. The people will riot; opportunists everywhere will jostle for the throne. It will be civil war on an unprecedented scale. The barbarians will find the Empire in such disarray that they will overrun us. His 'Golden Age' will be an age of slavery and destruction!"

Eclectus asked, "You say remove him - how?"

Pertinax paused to think. He turned to Marcia. "He trusts you above all others. You must poison his food, or his wine. That is the simplest way." There was another pause. "When he is dead, you will announce that he succumbed to an apoplectic fit and that he named me as his successor on his deathbed."

Laetus was alarmed. "How can we kill him? The soldiers and people love him. They will blame us for his death, no matter what we say!"

Pertinax was trying to be sure of himself: "No, not if you say he died from natural causes. The soldiers will follow my lead. I am the only one in Rome with enough authority to keep order. I will protect you. "

Eclectus wondered, "What if the truth leaks out? What if it is discovered that he was assassinated?"

Pertinax answered, "Pray that does not happen. But if it does, say that he was planning to have the gladiators kill all the leading men in Rome. That will at least get the senators behind you. Say that the funeral pyre was intended for his victims - and that you found a list of them with your names at the very top. No one will blame you for saving yourselves. But you must remember not to implicate me. Say that you pleaded with me after his death to take command and that I only agreed reluctantly. That is the only way I will be able to keep order and save you from the mob."

———

Within six months, Pertinax, Marcia, Eclectus, and Laetus had been killed and the Roman Empire was plunged into a civil war from which it would never fully recover.

———

According to history, Nerva died from the effects of a temper tantrum. Trajan faced death in a state of depression, believing he was being poisoned, Hadrian in mental and physical agony, and Antoninus ranting about recalcitrant kings. Marcus Aurelius faced death with resignation – reportedly banishing his attendants - and even his son - so they would not get his disease.

How did Commodus die? What were his last thoughts as he found himself wrapped in Narcissus' muscular embrace? Did he struggle against his powerful assailant? If so, it was of no avail. Despite all his athletic training, Commodus had the body of a philosopher.

Books by Jasper Burns

Commodus and the Five Good Emperors (Pietas Publications, 2012)

Turtle Crossing (Pietas Publications, 2012)

Dreamweaving (Pietas Publications, 2012)

Roman Empresses (Pietas Publications, 2012)

Wisdom Illustrated (Pietas Publications, 2012)

Fossil Beach (Pietas Publications, 2012)

Bulla Felix: The Roman Robin Hood (Pietas Publications, 2011)

Irish Hammered Pennies of Edward IV and Richard III

(Pietas Publications, 2009)

Great Women of Imperial Rome: Mothers and Wives of the Caesars

(Routledge, 2007)

Fossil Dreams (Pietas Publications, 2007)

Selected Lives: The Autobiography of a Soul (Pietas Publications, 2006)

Vipsania: A Roman Odyssey (Pietas Publications, 2006)

Trilobites: Common Trilobites of North America (NatureGuide Books, 2000)

Exploring Fossils (Virginia Museum of Natural History, 1998)

Fossil Collecting in the Mid-Atlantic States

(Johns Hopkins University Press, 1991)

Screenplays by Jasper Burns

Tiberius and Vipsania: A Roman Odyssey, WGA 146019, 2009

Bulla Felix: The Roman Robin Hood, WGA 1435345, 2011

Dreamweaving, WGA 1417962, 2010